To Harris v. _____,

Best wishes

Mary E. Peters

MARY P. *Autobiography*

Mary P.

Autobiography

Mary Peters with Ian Wooldridge

Stanley Paul, London

Stanley Paul & Company Ltd
3 Fitzroy Square, London W1

An Imprint of the Hutchinson Publishing Group

London Melbourne Sydney Auckland
Wellington Johannesburg Cape Town
and agencies throughout the world

First published 1974
© Mary Peters 1974

Set in Monotype Ehrhardt

Printed in Great Britain by
R. & R. Clark Ltd, Brandon Street
Edinburgh

ISBN 0 09 122280 X

To BUSTER

Contents

Acknowledgments

Many people and organisations have given us time, advice and help in compiling this book. We would particularly like to thank Charlie Stewart, Mel Watman, Neil Allen, Roy Moor, Margaret McShane, the *Belfast Telegraph*, Lord Rupert Nevill, Ulster Television, BBC Northern Ireland, Rowel Friers and Les Jones.

Photograph Credits

Associated Newspapers/Associated Press/Belfast Telegraph/ Colorsport/Gerry Cranham / Daily Express / Tony Duffy / Independent Newspapers Ltd / Irish Times/E. D. Lacey/Walter McEvoy/John C. Parker/Press Association/Syndication International / United Press International / Xth British Commonwealth Games Organizing Committee.

Foreword

Any book by or about Mary Peters would be incomplete without references to certain terrible events which have occurred in Belfast and elsewhere. They have contributed to the shaping of her remarkable character as much as the gruelling months and years spent in lonely training to become the greatest woman athlete of her time. For reasons which will become obvious to the perceptive reader there are incidents and issues about which it would not only be unwise for Mary to comment but actually unsafe. Nevertheless this book would be a fake if it were to ignore them. I have therefore adopted a simple device in preparing it for publication. All the words in normal type are Mary's own words, spoken into a tape-recorder and merely edited by me. All the words in italic type are my own comment, observations or description. I and I alone am responsible for them. They were gleaned during several visits to Northern Ireland and its beleaguered capital where Mary continues to live by choice because of her affection for its Catholics, its Protestants and those who know no God at all.

IAN WOOLDRIDGE
Belfast, August 1974

Prologue

The dawn didn't break that Sunday morning in Munich. 'Break' suggests that it suddenly snatched you out of a long, dreamless sleep and you get up rested and relaxed and start planning a pleasant day. For me, alone in my one-roomed flatlet high up in those towering white blocks of the Olympic Village, the dawn didn't break at all. It started seeping in slowly down the sides of the curtains and, God knows, it had taken long enough coming. In fact I'd been lying there waiting for it all night. I must have dozed, for ten minutes here and there I suppose, but I don't remember it. Every time I switched the light on to look at my watch it seemed that the hands had moved backwards. Every time I couldn't help seeing the cards and good-luck telegrams stacked around the room and my mind went racing away again. There wasn't a sound outside. There were nearly 12 000 souls in that Village and a couple of million out there in the great city beyond it and they were all sleeping but me. You can work yourself up with sheer nerves and envy about an injustice like that but the night wasn't without its ironic humour. Rosemary Stirling had promised to wake me at half past seven in case I *overslept*. I could have read the entire works of Tolstoy by then.

Instead I just lay there reliving every second of the previous day. The 100 metres hurdles, the shot and the high jump were done and I was leading the field. Two events, the hated long jump and the 200 metres, were still to come. The trouble with the pentathlon isn't so much the running and jumping and throwing as the night in between. When it's the Olympic Games and you're ahead and you've lived and dreamed of this day for twenty years this night is as long as a generation. I tossed and turned and turned and tossed and when I gave in and got up the bed looked like a bundle of laundry.

I went across to the window and drew back the curtains. It was grey and misty and damp outside with no hint of the blazing day to come. My kit was already laid out on the second bed. I am very meticulous about things like that. The condemned lady did not eat a hearty breakfast. I brewed up some coffee on one of the electric rings and ate the yoghurt which I had brought up from the rest-aurant the previous evening when I had come to bed at about ten thirty. I wondered how the opposition had slept. I knew exactly who the opposition were. There was Burglinde Pollak, very blonde and very Iron Curtain trained, from East Germany. She was the world record holder for the pentathlon and she was lying second, right on my heels. Curiously, to those not *au fait* with the mathe-matical intricacies of time and motion on the athletics track, I was far more concerned about the opponent lying fifth. Heide Rosendahl, with her studious look and her steel-rimmed spectacles, may not strike the uninitiated as epitomising feminine power in sport but I was well acquainted with her character and knew her to be a stupen-dous long jumper and fabulous sprinter. There was another factor, too. Heide was representing West Germany. She was the local girl performing before an idolatrous crowd and when they shouted I knew that that great rising roar would pick her up and lift her as never before. Crowd power should never be underestimated. It's why so many football teams win at home.

It was a thoughtful breakfast but no more than that. I was terribly tense but I wasn't nervous because the issue was very clear. The bronze medal, to me, was worthless. So was the silver. It had to be gold or nothing. I wanted it for me. I wanted it for my coach, Buster McShane. Above all I wanted it for the people back home who would be watching me that day on television. I didn't mean the people of England. Back home was Belfast and Northern Ireland where it was long overdue for something good to happen. 'Mary P', I said, which is what all my close friends call me, 'you can't let those people down.'

It may sound a little trite and sentimental now but down that long night I had time to get my priorities clear.

We went down in the lift and out into the morning. The mist and the greyness had gone. The sun was rising in a clear sky and glinting already off that dragon's back roof of the Olympic Stadium. In there I would prevail or fail and by sunset, for better or for worse, it would be all over. The longest day was about to follow the longest night of my life.

1. First Steps

Coming in from the airport it is hard to recognise Belfast as a British city. As you come round one bend, with the cranes and chimney stacks still far below to the right, the taxi driver says: 'A lot of bodies have been dumped here.' His voice is dull and resigned. Soon you are down among the shoddy streets with the all too familiar names. Shankill, Crumlin, the Falls, Unity Flats. They remind you of a mouthful of broken teeth. The gaps are where buildings, often corner pubs, have been bombed out of existence. There are barriers and concrete roadblocks and barbed wire and, here and there, a defiant sectarian flag. Soldiers in flak jackets, with their fingers crooked in the trigger guards of automatic machine guns, lean against walls. They look incredibly young. Massive posters on hoardings bear a telephone number which the public is invited to call to report anything suspicious 'in complete confidence'. You must love a city to distraction, you think, to live here by choice. Mary Peters lives in a tall, rather forbidding house along the Antrim Road. The taxi driver doesn't need to be told the address. He knows it already. 'She's a folk hero' he says and talks about the day of her homecoming. The way he talks she could be his daughter. He leans across from his driver's seat to wave at Mary as she opens the door of the house with no number.

My accent doesn't tell the truth at all because there isn't a single drop of Irish blood in my veins. I was born in Halewood, on the out-skirts of Liverpool, and both my father and mother were born near there too. We weren't even Liverpool-Irish. All four of my grand-parents were English so by birth I'm pure Lancashire. A Scouse, in fact, though I had never even heard that word before I left. It was the nomadic life of the insurance world that made us reverse the trend and move from Liverpool to Northern Ireland. My father was an agent selling insurance for the Liverpool Victoria Friendly Society and three years after the war he was promoted to inspector in the Belfast area. For nearly two years he lived and worked there on his own, just coming back to Liverpool once every fortnight to see how we were getting on. He did that, as he did everything, out of a sense of responsibility to us. He was desperately ambitious for his children. My brother, John, had just won his way through to a new school and my father had the kind of selflessness to put up with that lonely, chaotic life so that his only son's education shouldn't be interrupted at a critical period.

I loved my father dearly. The only problem, until we moved to join him in Ireland, was that I didn't know him at all. We lived in classic, comfortable suburbia in a neat semi-detached with a neat garden and a bed of lupins at the side of the house which were so magnificent that people used to stop to admire them. It's little enough to remember about one's early life but we didn't do those spectacular things which stick in the memory. I only know that my father was never there. At first, in the war years, he worked by day and fire-watched by night. Even afterwards the only time I really spent with him was on Saturday mornings when he sat down to make up his books for the week. I would sit there in the same room, pretending to write in my own book, but actually looking at him. He worked and I watched and, somehow, that summed up the relationship between us. There was protection on his side and admiration on mine but there was absolutely no communication between us.

I was extremely close to my mother who was the kind of practical lady who never throws away a torn sheet but sews it into tea-towels and aprons. But she was almost the only feminine influence on my life out of school. There were no girls in our street, only boys. I had no sisters, only one brother. I became a tomboy.

Pianists always seem to be able to recall exactly when and where they struck their first note and actors the incident which fired them to take to the stage. Quite often the talent was hereditary. This wasn't so in my case. We had no sporting traditions at all in my entire family and I don't remember either of my parents being interested. There was, a little later, to be a moment to which I can now look back and say 'That was when I became an athlete.' But a psychiatrist might see it differently. Even during those first twelve years in Liverpool certain characteristics were emerging which are essential to the personality of the competitor. No one can teach them and few would want to, perhaps, because they are not necessarily the traits one would want to instil in a child.

There was, for example, a streak of exhibitionism. I detest show-offs and braggarts now, but I can recall showing off like mad in front of the neighbours who used to stop to gaze at our lupins. I had become pretty adept with a skipping rope and Mary P was never abashed at putting on a free show in the front garden for the passers-by. There was also an increased determination when prizes were involved such as at the school swimming gala where the reward for winning the width of the bath race was a sixpenny savings stamp. Unlike the Olympic Games the prizes weren't distributed on the spot and I can remember going to knock on the headmistress's door every day for a week after that to see whether my prize had come through.

There was, too, an altogether darker side which emerged the day we were leaping into a sand pit, which is about the most accurate way I can describe the first long jump competition in which I ever took part. I was probably eight at the time and my big rival was a girl called Pauline whose face remains as clear to me today as Rosendahl's or Pollak's. Pauline was ahead of me but then got sand in her eyes and had to withdraw. My reactions were hardly those expounded by the Baron de Coubertin when he revived the modern Olympics and summoned the youth of the world to gather in an atmosphere of noble purpose and good sportsmanship. Far from it. 'Goodie,' I said to myself. 'Now maybe I shall win.'

But the tomboy environment was probably what counted most. There were no girls at birthday parties to insist we played with dolls. It was always races, organised by my mother, in the field at the back of the house. Then there was the nightly contest against the bus that brought us home from school. The bus stop was seventy yards away from our house and we used to jump off and sprint away, with our satchels thumping up and down on our backs, to reach our front gate before the driver could accelerate past us. Later, when my brother proved himself the brains of the family and got through to grammar shool with its organised sport there were cross-country runs in the evenings. He must have many memories of the small figure stumbling breathlessly after him crying 'Wait for me.'

*During the two years when her father was commuting between Liver-
pool and Northern Ireland, Mary Peters paid her first visit to Belfast.
It was not the start of the love affair. She spent a few days there over
Easter and remembers it now only for its 'strangeness' and tasting the
first milk-shake of her life. This was not yet the era of the package-deal
holiday which has brought Torremolinos and Tangier and Rimini into
the conversation range of small children from all income groups. The
Peters family spent their annual holidays in the Isle of Man or Scarborough. Belfast, though barely a few miles to the west, was a new world.
The prospect of living there, to an 11-year-old girl, was not appealing.
Her affinity with Northern Ireland and its people, therefore, does not go
back to the evening when she sat on the stairs of her Liverpool home and
eavesdropped on a conversation between her parents.*

It was a sneaky thing to do, I suppose, but I had this instinct that
something big was about to happen to all of us. It proved to be right.
My father had been promoted again, this time as area manager to
Ballymena. My brother was launched on a grammar shool education
and I had failed my eleven-plus so there was nothing to stop us from
moving and being united again as a family. I looked forward to that
but even as my father said that we would now be moving I had this
feeling that it was going to be a traumatic experience. That proved
to be right as well. Ballymena is north of Belfast, up under the left-
hand shoulder of the Mountains of Antrim. We arrived there just
before Christmas with four days of the school term left. It was
decided that I might as well start classes right away and to my
horror I found that I literally couldn't understand what anyone was
talking about. The accent was as bewildering to me as a child from
the deep south of England would have found it had he been trans-
ported overnight to the Orkneys. In those early days I had to have
someone sitting beside me in class to interpret the lessons.

But if they were strange to me I, clearly, was even stranger to
them in my St Trinian's hat and double-breasted crombie overcoat.
I was 'the English girl', an object of curiosity. I suppose most of us
crave for some kind of identification that will separate us from the
masses and it was at that Model School in Ballymena that I found it
though, at first, it required no effort on my part. But I thrived on it.
My earliest excursion into competitive sport there didn't quite make
the headlines because though I won the sack race I was subsequently

disqualified for jumping the gun. But within a few months the tomboy years back in Liverpool had paid off and I won the junior
championships in the school sports. Academically, too, my confidence had grown. Moving to Ireland gave me a second chance at a
scholarship and this time I won my way through to join my brother
at Ballymena Academy where I was searchingly examined for my
intellectual capacity, placed in the lower stream and was blissfully
happy for two years. Liverpool and England were forgotten.

Looking back I realise it to have been an important period, for
when our next move came I was prepared for it. I was no longer the
nonentity of the sprawling suburbs of Liverpool. I was good at sport
and I was totally accepted in Northern Ireland. So when my father
was transferred to Portadown, and my brother and I were moved to
Portadown College, I hurled myself into every activity there was:
the Hockey Club, the Film Society, the Debating Society, the Dancing Club and the Athletic Club. I was never home before six in the
evenings and still faced a pile of homework because examinations
didn't come easily. But it was never a strain. We were taught that
everything in life was an adventure, that everything had to be tried,
that every hour had to be lived to the utmost, that discussion was
better than dogma. For this I was, and still am, indebted to a remarkable educationist and headmaster, Mr Woodman. I loved him
as I loved my father. In fact, if I had a personal problem I would
take it to him before I took it to my father.

*Like Mary Peters herself, Donald J. Woodman has no Irish ancestry.
He is a Londoner, born in Willesden, who taught at Kilburn Grammar
School before serving as a Royal Navy telegraphist during the war. His
Irish wife found the anonymity of London stifling so they returned to
Northern Ireland. Today he lives in retirement in a semi-detached house
on the outskirts of Portadown. He is a slim, benign 'Mr Chips' whose
small study is lined from carpet to ceiling with authors from Cicero to
R. L. Stevenson and the career records of the 3000 pupils who came
under his influence. One of them, Mary Peters, he made Head Girl.
Some of his concepts will today be seen as quite unexceptional. In the
context of their time, and particularly their place, they were revolu-
tionary. He recognised the embarrassment of six foot schoolboys wearing
school caps. He allowed them to go bareheaded. He calculated that
150 of his pupils were smoking on the sly. He called a school meeting at*

B

which it was decided that provided they would listen to anti-smoking propaganda and had their parents' permission they could smoke at school between stipulated hours in a certain room. Several years and much scientific evidence later he believes his decision was wrong and does not hesitate to say so. Donald Woodman himself has never smoked in his life.

Mr Woodman had 600 pupils in his school at any given time and whether we were first-formers or prefects he knew every one of us by name. His methods were encouragement and persuasion. He even encouraged me to continue with Latin. He also made the decision, quite abruptly, which was to take me round the world as an athlete.

Sport was an haphazard business at Portadown, especially for girls. One afternoon, in the fourth year, I was standing by the boundary of a field where a number of girls were being instructed in the arts of cricket, which appealed to me about as much as Latin and struck me as being even less useful in whatever life lay out ahead. Wistfully I was looking through a hole in the hedge to the next field where an exclusively male group of about a dozen were taking athletics. This was not the Athletics Club. It was the school squad being coached and drilled and disciplined like some crack squad of guardsmen. It was typical of my headmaster that he saw my envious glance, interpreted it and acted. He simply led me through the gap in the hedge, broke down the barriers of male chauvinism fully twenty years before anyone had even heard of the phrase and said to the coach, 'Let Mary join you.' Kenny McClelland showed no surprise or irritation. He had been a pupil at the school and was back as a student teacher. Today he is the vice-principal of a school some twenty miles from Belfast and I am delighted at his success. I owe him much, for that afternoon I took the first short step along the road to Munich.

2. *A Potential Star*

The making of an athlete today is a solemn, scientific process involving doctors, dieticians, intensive coaching and stupendous expenditure. To show athletic promise in East Germany by the age of nine is to be caught up in an Orwellian machine geared to mass producing gold medals a decade later. Other Eastern bloc countries, America and Australia – whether for reasons of national prestige or parental ambition – have all been guilty in certain instances of dehumanising their young in the manic pursuit of Olympic honours. One factor in these countries is always taken for granted: the availability of tracks, gymnasia and equipment. Northern Ireland, circa 1954, could not be accused of preaching a similar philosophy.

Our immediate neighbour in Portadown was Mr Gordon, a kind and encouraging man who owned the field behind our house and let us use it for our training. From early on he took a close interest in my progress as an athlete, even to the point where he promised to buy a goat to keep the grass short in our personal stadium. The deal was that I had to promise to drink the goat's milk to replace the calories I was burning up every evening. I couldn't face it so he never bought the goat. But he never stopped us training or acting out our sporting fantasies on his land. It wasn't quite a Tartan track but my debt to him can never be repaid.

Usually there were three of us: my brother, who was desperately keen on athletics but never seemed to win much, myself and Kenny McClelland. Kenny was now something rather more than the student teacher to whom I had originally been introduced through a hole in the hedge. We were madly in love. At least we thought we were madly in love. He was two or three years older than me but that was rather cancelled out by the fact that, in stature, I towered above him. He only came up to my shoulder and it was only subsequently that I learned that our very tender, very platonic relationship caused a certain amount of amusement around the town. We must have been an odd looking couple but we were almost inseparable. We never went to the cinema together because we had no need to. Athletics was our cause and it brought us together with everyone's approval. Here again I was lucky; as a coach, Kenny was years ahead of his time.

We ran everywhere we could find a flat stretch of land including, for a short while, the Portadown Golf Club. We were given special permission for that but unfortunately it was revoked. Apparently my brother's startling white track suit put the more dedicated golfers off their stroke. We were asked to leave. I hope those golfers won't think badly about their decision now. Northern Ireland at that time didn't place quite the same importance on athletics as, say, the University of Southern California. If you wanted to train you had to find your own facilities and if you wanted equipment you had to cadge it or make it. My technique was to tell Kenny what we needed and then Kenny would go to my father and tell him it was vitally important for the advancement of my athletics career. That's how, on the day I was fifteen, I received from my father the somewhat unusual birthday present of two tons of sand. A lorry came and dumped it in our neighbour's drive and we had to hi-jack a wheelbarrow to shift it into Mr Gordon's field before he came home in his car. John, Kenny, my father and I then dug a pit, shovelled the sand into it and thus built our own long jump area.

Our high jump facilities weren't exactly Olympic standard, either. We got a couple of broom handles, hammered nails into them and found a long piece of bamboo to use as the bar. This was later replaced by some really smart high jump stands which my father bought for me. He was terribly ambitious for us and gave us many things but his misfortune was that there was no end to it because, unknowingly, I was heading to become a pentathlete.

I didn't even know what the pentathlon was when I was first invited to compete in one. Kenny had to explain to me that it was a combination of five events, two of which – the hurdles and the shot – were absolutely unknown to me. Neither was in even the school athletics curriculum so my long-suffering father had to use his ingenuity all over again to shape some now rather important equipment out of the kind of everyday objects you find lying around small Irish towns. The hurdles proved to be no real problem. They just needed a lot of broom handles and a lot of bamboo. But the shot raised real difficulties. In the end a local foundry shaped a wooden ball exactly the size a shot had to be and then had it cast. To this day I cannot work out how they managed to get a shot of the regulation size to weigh the regulation eight pounds thirteen and two-fifths ounces.

Armed with a shot I now needed something more practical than a rude answer when I asked where I was going to put it. You don't learn much just flinging a shot around an open field. So at the back of the house we tied a nail to a piece of string and scraped out the correctly sized throwing circle while my father made a stop board, the wooden kerb at the front of the circle which you are not allowed to touch or pass over while in the act of putting. At first I putted there, on the grass, in spikes. Then we discovered that while that was the general practice in Ireland, international rules permitted you to throw off a concrete base. My father reacted heroically to the discovery. More sand and some cement suddenly appeared and he was back in the building business again, constructing a throwing area as firm as an airport runway. It is a small commentary on the athletics story of the country when I add that that was the first concrete shot-putting circle in the whole of Northern Ireland. It is still there today.

By discovering the pentathlon I turned to two new athletics events which ultimately turned out to be my best. It is the best argument I know for encouraging youngsters to try their hands at absolutely everything in sport before they settle for a single specialist event. There is no other way of discovering their potential. I only came across the shot by asking Kenny what a pentathlon was, yet very shortly after taking it up I was equalling, then breaking, the Northern Ireland all-comers' record. It had to be the all-comers' record because, since I had been born in Liverpool, I was not permitted to hold native records. Practically every time I competed I was adding an extra couple of inches to my previous best performance and within six months of getting that heavy black ball from the foundry I really was quite good at throwing it.

Obviously I was doing most of my running and jumping at school but the real, hard, tough experience was being gained outside.

Almost every Saturday, somewhere in Northern Ireland, they were holding open meetings where all-comers of all ages and sizes and temperaments could compete. This was a tough, colourful world which has almost disappeared, but at the time its lessons were as valuable to the rising athlete as, say, the experience of booth-boxing was to the rising professional fighter. My father took me to dozens of these small meetings all over the country. Kenny would come along with advice and more often than not we would go home loaded with small prizes. I loved collecting these trinkets, if only to give them to my mother. She could almost have set up as a wholesaler in sets of teaspoons and salt and pepper sets but she would never part with any of them. I can recall how terribly upset she was when she chipped an ornate oval plate which I had won for some event or other in a meeting at Newcastle, County Down. To me it was nothing more than a plate which kept breadcrumbs off the table-cloth. To her it was a *trophy* which her daughter had won.

These were marvellous meetings with all the classically Irish atmosphere which one associates with county-town fairs and the make-your-own-fun of Irish life in the days before TV and rising living standards killed most of them off. They varied enormously in size and importance. In Lisburn you would find yourself sprinting on very bumpy grass where the lanes had been marked off by pieces of string instead of the usual white lines. In Londonderry once, at a meeting which my father had seen advertised in the newspapers, I found myself running against factory girls wearing things like tennis shorts and sun-tops. I had proper shorts and proper spikes and I was so embarrassed about it that I didn't want to run at all. But my father wasn't driving all that way for nothing so I had to take part. I won absolutely everything. I even ran a 440 yards, which would have killed me when I became an international athlete, and I won that, too.

One of the really big ones was the Royal Ulster Constabulary Sports at Balmoral Stadium, Belfast. There were bands and gymnastic displays and the highlight always came when the police cadets used to march out and form up to make the letters RUC. It was a great day out with enormous crowds but even here, at the athletic event of the Ulster year, the running surface was so uneven that I suppose most of today's big names would regard it as something beneath their dignity to compete on it. I ran and loved it. My parents were there and so was Kenny, to talk to me with all the earnestness of a world-renowned coach before a race and then hold my hand like a rather proud boy friend afterwards. We really were terribly fond of one another.

It was in one of these larger meetings in Belfast that I first ran against Thelma Hopkins, who was then a star British international. I couldn't believe how quiet and unassuming, even shy, she was. Although I was certainly three, possibly four years younger, she found it quite difficult to say anything more than 'Hello' until we had known one another for quite some time. Mostly we were competing in handicap races in which I would be given ten or twelve yards advantage. Occasionally I would beat her and it did my standing at school no harm at all when I could say, 'Oh yes, I beat Thelma Hopkins,' carefully neglecting to add that it had been a handicap race. Thelma and I were to become very good friends but, in those early days, she was sheer inspiration. I competed against her on the day she broke the world high jump record in Belfast in 1956. The London Olympiads had come over for a match against Belfast University at the Queen's University athletic ground at Cherryvale but there was also an open competition as well. The high jump, with its cinder approach and soft landing, was sheer luxury after Mr Gordon's field. I had finished jumping at 4 ft 8 in before Thelma actually started and then I lay there in awe as the bar went higher and higher and she finally went over at 5 ft 8½ in, adding half an inch to the world record which had been set up in Kiev two years earlier by Miss Chudina of Russia. Thelma, in fact, was to hold that record for only two months before it went back behind the Iron Curtain again, but the thrill of having actually competed in the same event was to have a big influence on my determination to break out of the country town circuit and see the world through sport. Anyway, my 4 ft 8 in was enough to see me finish fourth to a world record. Kenny and I went back to Mr Gordon's field with visions of glory and the sounds of acclaim in our ears for we were now in contact with the mighty. Thelma was just off to compete in the Olympics.

Fame is relative. Mary Peters, the tenderfoot competitor in the big meetings in Belfast, was swiftly becoming a celebrity at school. Her name was regularly appearing in the newspapers. By fifteen she was already being described in one as 'a potential star.' She remained,

according to Donald Woodman, her headmaster, 'a model of modesty.'
He made her head girl. At home she was beginning to compile her first
press cuttings book. She had a habit of underlining her name in ink
wherever it appeared in the small-print used to tabulate results. One
of the earliest clipped out photographs is of Thelma Hopkins winning a
sprint. A large inked arrow points to a tiny figure in the background
and Mary, indignant at the caption writer's oversight, has written
'Mary Peters' in large letters in the margin. Inevitably she totally
dominated her school's athletics and some of her times and distances, at
various ages, will be of interest to younger readers currently developing
as athletes. It is important to remember that Mary's was essentially a
do-it-yourself training, bereft of the many facilities and opportunities
now taken for granted even in Britain. At the age of fourteen, as a
school intermediate, she broke both the intermediate and senior school
records for the high jump with 4 ft 5 in. She also won the long jump
with 13 ft 10 in. The following summer, still an intermediate, she swept
the board in all four major track and field events: first in the 100 yards
in 12·3 seconds, first in the 220 yards in 30·4 seconds, first in the high
jump, again with 4 ft 5 in, and first in the long jump which she had now
lengthened to 14 ft 11 in. Her astounding achievement in that same
summer, however, was her performance in open competition at the
Ballymena Athletic Club in her first ever pentathlon. Against a field
of ten which included the two Olympians, Miss Hopkins and Maeve
Kyle, Mary came third to the two major stars and was, in fact, only
just beaten out of second place by the vastly experienced Mrs Kyle.
The final scores, under the old points-scoring system, were: Thelma
Hopkins 3723 points, Maeve Kyle 3324, Mary Peters 3253. Mary ran
the 80 metres hurdles in 15·5 seconds, the 200 metres in 28 seconds,
finished equal second in the high jump with 4 ft 8¼ in and, throwing the
shot in public for the first time, achieved 27 ft 4½ in. There is no record
of her distance in the long jump. 'I was probably too far behind for it
to have been counted,' she suggests. Mary, undoubtedly, was on the way.
The days were full of sunlight and friendship and the earth was at her
feet. But the idyll could not last for there was about to occur a traumatic
experience which was to threaten the whole security of her existence and
cause her to question, not for the last time, the meaning of religious faith.

Death was always something that happened to other people in other
families. For me it had no meaning or dimension and because of

Above: In the garden of the house where I was born in Halewood near Liverpool with my brother John in the foreground. I used to bounce up and down in the pram until I fell into the rosebed, so Mum had tied a brick on to the handle.

Right: An early photograph taken of a family holiday in Scarborough.

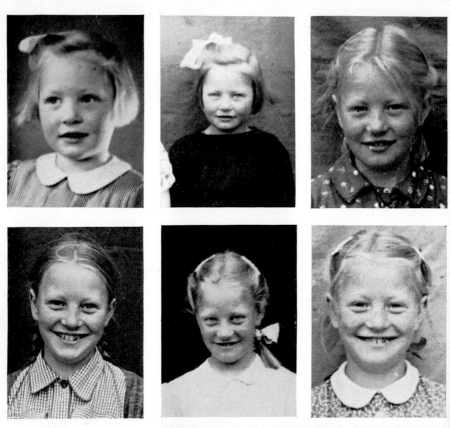

Above: The development of the smile.

Right: And a big grin on my face winning a sack race. To my great disappointment I was disqualified because the starter said I had jumped the gun. I went back and told him he should have stopped the race because even at that age (about 11) I knew that he was at fault and not me.

Above: High-jumping in the field behind our house. You can see the nails in the broom handle, and a bamboo cane as the cross-bar. I used to just run and land on grass.

Left: Victory in the high jump at Ballymena in 1951. I went on to win the 'Junior Shield' for the best all-round athlete.

Below left: This is an unusual photograph taken at Trinity College in Dublin. The officials wore toppers and tails and in the background is Ulick O'Connor, the famous Irish barrister and journalist with the *Daily Mirror*.

Above: A school photograph showing me as headgirl with Mr Woodman on my left.

Left: I took part in my first British pentathlon championship in 1956, coming second behind Margaret Rowley with Alma Osborne third. You can see I had rolled up my shorts because they were so much longer than the others'.

this I was utterly unprepared for my mother's death, slow and
distressing though it was. I was very close to her and loved her
deeply and she was such a gentle woman, with her shyness and
modesty and her perfect skin and the lovely hair that stretched right
down to her waist when she unplaited it, that I could not visualise
an existence without her there. She fell ill in the summer of 1956,
not long after I had competed in the Belfast meeting in which
Thelma Hopkins had broken the world record. We were all on
holiday in a caravan at Newcastle, when she began to suffer from
severe swelling of the feet. My father had no faith in doctors at
all, always believing that they were more interested in golf than
in curing people. But by the time my mother was taken into
hospital in Belfast for exploratory tests there was nothing any
doctor could do anyway. I suppose I was the only person either in
the hospital or in our family who did not realise that she had cancer.
Astonishing though it will seem to any teenager of today, I had
never heard the word cancer. It was not then the subject of endless
television documentaries and newspaper articles. It was still a
dreaded word that was kept in the dark and it explains much about
the sheltered existence we led that had I been told that that was
what my mother was suffering from I would, in my innocence, have
asked whether or not it was serious. I think my mother herself tried
to warn me about what was going to happen. I knitted her a royal
blue twin-set and she said 'No, you have it because I might never
be able to wear it.' I refused to understand the words and I refused
to understand what was happening when she became steadily heavier
with gathering fluid and was then taken over to Liverpool to see
Grandma Peters and the family for the last time and then returned
to our home where a nurse was brought in to tend her. She had been
terribly burned by radium treatment for stomach cancer but the
sheer optimism and happiness of my life until then still left me
quite defenceless when she died four months later, in the early
hours of New Year's Eve. I stood for a long while staring at her
face which, in death, was still beautiful and reflected the goodness
and gentleness of her character. She was buried in Liverpool, five
days later, beside her father and mother. I felt very alone.
   What followed was a deeply emotionally disturbed period of
several months during which I failed to come to terms with another
woman replacing my mother in our home. I write it, frankly,

because the wounds have long since healed and I recognise, now, that the shortcomings were mine. At the time the arrival of Doris Waterhouse, who had been my mother's bridesmaid and was my godmother, was more than I could cope with. I scarcely knew her because she had lived in Canada for many years but my father asked me to write to her informing her of my mother's death. She arrived in Liverpool on the evening after the funeral and my father asked her to come over to Ireland as our housekeeper. She did so a few weeks later and though I baked pies and laid out the dining table beautifully to greet her, I could not forgive her simply for not being my mother. I was quick to resent the immediate ordering of a washing machine, whereas my mother had always had to make do with a washboard and mangle. My father would take her out on drives to some of the beauty spots of Northern Ireland and although they always asked me to go with them, I would refuse. Shopping trips to Belfast were agony. I would see my father take Doris's elbow to cross a street while I came trailing along behind. I had no resentment of Doris as a person, only for the position which circumstances had seen her assume. But I resisted her warmth and kindness and in doing so I know I caused not a little distress. My father either did not understand my feelings or else reasoned that time would work them out of my system without any interference from him. It was a difficult time for us all.

My father and Doris Waterhouse were married in a little country church outside Portadown six months after my mother's death. The ceremony took place at eight o'clock on a June morning and my brother and I were witnesses. We then all went into Armagh city for the reception. Eight people were there, including the bride and bridegroom, the minister and the very fat, very red-faced, very jolly taxi driver. That summer, athletically, was not a very good one for me.

All the protective barriers were tumbling at once. My brother had moved away to Stranmillis Training College and it was fast approaching the time when I had to leave school where, as a good athlete and head girl, I had enjoyed the happiness and popularity that had come from being something of a success. My father and Mr Woodman both virtually took it for granted that I would become a physical education teacher. It seemed such an obvious choice that they even got the application forms for me to fill in. But again I defied the two people I admired the most. I reasoned that very few PE teachers ever came through as sports stars and, anyway, I loved the domestic side, though was less good at the scientific aspects of domestic science. I applied for a place at the Domestic Science College in Belfast, and resplendent in a new suit from C & A's, and armed with such invaluable advice as 'Don't cross your legs', I went or an interview.

A few weeks previously I had taken part in a *Down Your Way* programme when Franklin Engelmann had visited Portadown and this appeared to be worth at least ten marks in the opinion of one of the interviewers who had heard it. Another caught me on the trickier subject of literature which, as an outdoor tomboy, had never loomed very large in my life.

'What sort of books do you read?' he asked. I groped around wildly and suddenly clutched the name of Dickens out of mid-air. 'Do you mean to say,' he said, 'that if I gave you a copy of *The Cruel Sea* and a copy of *Bleak House* you would choose the Dickens?' 'Yes I would,' I said, and I was probably speaking the truth. So close and confined had been my small world in Portadown that, at the time, I had never heard of either *The Cruel Sea* or Nicholas Monsarrat.

I apparently impressed them that at least I had a future over a sewing-maching or a hot stove. I came through the interview successfully, and it signalled the end of family life. My father and step-mother sold their house and moved to England, later to follow my brother to Sydney, Australia. I moved into Belfast, a city with faults and blemishes like every other city, but a city which made me welcome when I needed love very badly.

3. The Big League

It was with Mary's encouragement, rather than with her permission, that I interviewed a number of her colleagues and friends about certain aspects of her character. If we were all together at the time she would say 'Go on, tell him the truth' and then leave the room. She had no desire to collaborate on a book which would be a mass of athletics statistics or portray her as a blonde paragon. Nor did she reserve the right to censor or amend any of the remarks made independently about her. Don McBride, a pale, thin, highly articulate Northern Ireland sprinter, trained with Mary for the greater part of their track careers. He was a practising Christian and confessed that he was occasionally distressed at the alacrity with which she could command some extremely colourful barrack-room language if anything went wrong. 'Also,' he said, 'she always seemed to know the latest blue story which she would proceed to tell quite brilliantly.' McBride went on to say, 'I'm not sitting in judgement. If that's the worst you can find to say about a person then you are talking about someone quite exceptional. I suppose the explanation is that for almost the whole of her life as an athlete she was exposed predominantly to male company. There was always a lot of conjecture about why she never got married. I don't pretend to know the answer. What I do know is that Mary, for all her popularity and friends, has always struck me as being an isolated person. For example she knows people all over the world, but I doubt whether she knows very much about her immediate neighbours where she lives. She is the most completely self-sufficient person I've ever met. There's probably an explanation for it, but I don't know what it is.'

Coming to terms with the world when you've led a sheltered life in a backwater can lead to some difficult moments. Athletically I was making progress. I didn't need the Irish newspapers to tell me that.

But Northern Ireland is one place and England is the other side of the Pacific when you are suddenly chosen for your first 'overseas' trip. As I have said, the year following my mother's death was not exactly a sporting milestone but by the September I was going over to Birmingham University to compete in the 1956 British pentathlon championships. You would have thought we were emigrating forever. My brother came with me as a kind of chaperon and we went via Liverpool where we stayed with my grandmother overnight. The following night we spent in the Cobden Hotel in Birmingham. I could hardly sleep. I, Mary Peters, was *overseas*, staying in an *hotel*, about to compete in *national* championships. This is the point in the cinema where the heroine does something terribly sophisticated like falling in love and bringing a crowd of 100 000 to its feet by breaking about eight world records. My only concern was not to be late. In fact I was so concerned about it that we turned up at the Birmingham University track about an hour before any of the groundsmen. This was just as well. I simply couldn't find the changing rooms so I went to the groundsmen's hut and changed there, laying out my school uniform over a wheelbarrow. I was kitted out and ready for action roughly half a morning before anyone else arrived. Eventually the stars showed up. I knew their names, of course, and I suddenly found myself contemplating the ultimately glamorous figure of Margaret Rowley, pentathlete. She emerged wearing the dramatic all-black ensemble of Birchfield Harriers and was just the most dramatic lady I had ever seen. All at once I was conscious of the fact that my shorts came down almost to my knees. I hastily rolled them up about three turns, revealing some six inches of thigh which had not been exposed previously to the more conservative audiences of Ulster. It was a tremendous relief to see that there was one girl, whose name was something like Parrish or Parsons, who was even more nervous than I was. In the high jump she just couldn't bring herself to take off. She rocked and rolled on her feet for minutes on end and then broke away without jumping every time she reached the bar. There was a terrible moment when the University clock struck midday and seemed to go on for ever. Miss Parrish, or Parsons, wouldn't jump during the distraction and for a dreadful moment I thought the event was over. In fact it was only just starting and I was to do rather well. I finished second, only 133 points behind the gorgeous

Miss Rowley. I'd come fourth in the shot, fourth in the hurdles, second in the long jump and first in both the high jump and the 200 metres.

It was too late in the season to do much other than paste a sudden rash of newspaper cuttings in a rather bilious green-covered book bearing the imprint 'School and College Jotter issued by the Education Company Ltd of 36, Fountain Street, Belfast.' But soon the first fan-card was to arrive, addressed to the Blonde Bombshell. It didn't do any harm now that I was alone, living in digs and studying in Belfast. Now that my father was gone I was absolutely determined to show him what I could do. The first thing I did in the summer of 1957 was to smash the Northern Ireland shot record by miles only to be put right back in my place when it was discovered that the shot was considerably under weight. But the moment was only briefly delayed. In Ballymena, just after my eighteenth birthday, they weighed the shot beforehand to make certain it was legal and I then put it 34 ft 1 in, exactly one foot better than the previous Northern Ireland all-comers' record. As comparative performances went at the time, it was pretty good. By the end of that summer I was emerging quite well as a hurdler, a high jumper and a shot-putter.

But 1958 was to be the year. At the end of the summer, luring everyone to strive their utmost, were the Commonwealth Games in Cardiff. I knew that Northern Ireland would send only a small team but that I must stand a good chance of selection. What I needed was experience and that, in more aspects than one, was what I was about to get.

It must seem inconceivable to the child of the 70's to reach the age of eighteen before visiting London, but that's how it was for me. Even then it wasn't to go and see Westminster or the Crown Jewels but to get down to the White City, on the Wormwood Scrubbs side of Shepherds Bush, and run. We stayed in an hotel near Lancaster Gate, not quite overlooking Hyde Park but almost. It was around here that famous actresses and famous conductors and famous authors took their flats when they came to London, which was all very well to write home about but it was a very different story when I discovered that our hotel was teeming with famous athletes with whom, until now, my only connection was to cut their photographs out for inclusion in my scrapbook. I was terrified.

Inevitably I had little money. I had only just emerged from the days when my pocket money amounted to two shillings a week.

Thelma Hopkins was an angel. She took complete charge of me without patronising me at all. For the first time in my life I ate out in a restaurant where you didn't have to go along with a tray and select your own food. I was introduced to Chinese cooking complete with bean shoots, the most delicious things I had ever eaten. From time to time we took taxis. Thelma would pay for one and I would pay for the next. My taxi rides were agonising. I always had one eye on the fare-meter wondering if I would have enough money to pay for it. I would have been too scared to tell Thelma that I was flat broke. We managed somehow, until we came to the White City.

The event was the Women's AAA Championships and I was realistic enough to know that I didn't have a hope. I was here to gather experience and that is just what I got, even down to the point where a judge quietly informed me that my action in the shot-put was not only wrong but actually illegal. 'You must put it,' he said, 'not throw it.' I had to get it up under my chin. It didn't matter much. No one in the crowd had ever heard of me, no one expected me to do well and I duly obliged everyone's peace by making no impression at all on the meeting. I don't even know where I finished. But what I had learned was what it feels like to go into a stadium with people thronging through turnstiles and mixing with athletes who were household names and how to give your coat to a waiter in a restaurant and how much to tip a taxi-driver, provided you had the money, after a two mile journey. I think there should be educational courses to teach young people these things because it would save them far more embarrassment than being unable to conjugate a French irregular verb before a board of three schoolmasters who save up to take their families on a fortnight's package deal holiday to Dinard once every four years.

I returned to Belfast a wiser, if uncelebrated, young woman. But it was destined to be a good year. In the space of ten days, this time with a shot of the correct weight and also with a legal method, I broke the Northern Ireland record twice. The second time I increased it by ten inches. As it happened, in the final trials before the selection of the then Empire, now Commonwealth Games team, I added a further two feet to my distance but once again subsequent check-ups revealed that the shot I'd used had been too light. This sort of thing was becoming an Irish sick joke long before anyone had thought of the phrase.

It didn't matter much. When they came to name the four-woman Northern Ireland track and field team for Cardiff I was in it. There were Thelma Hopkins, Bridget Robinson, the javelin-thrower, Maeve Kyle and myself. Maeve was the only sprinter among us. The rest of us, essentially, were field-event performers but for reasons of prestige, as much as economics, we were asked if we would mind forming a 4 × 110 yards relay team to go in there and compete against the rest of the Commonwealth. It was rather like designating four glider pilots to fight the Battle of Britain.

There was much to learn, primarily that you don't go to a Commonwealth Games until you are officially kitted out. We were provided with gorgeous green blazers, complete with wire badges, and elegant white suits for the opening parade. These were so beautiful that it would have been nonsense to travel in them so we were asked to buy ourselves grey skirts for the journey. This is where a man like Mr Avery Brundage, by now President of the International Olympic Committee, was so desperately out of touch with the whole situation. He was so rich that he could have bought five million grey skirts, if that was what gave him a kick, without ever knowing the difference. As a first-year domestic science student I had to sit down and try to work out how I was going to buy one.

I did, as it happened, have a little money in my Post Office Savings book and I decided that if Northern Ireland could send me to the Games the least I could do was to show that I'd been touring abroad to places like Birmingham and London and come up with something smart. I went out and spent five pounds on the most beautiful, the very latest, the most elegant grey pleated skirt you ever saw. I was so thrilled about it that I came out of the store, went straight to a phone box and rang up Thelma Hopkins's mother, who was to be our team manager in Cardiff, to tell her about it. I spoke to her, put the receiver down, rushed out of the kiosk and had got all of fifty yards up the road when it dawned on me that I'd left the carrier bag containing the skirt by the telephone. I went straight back but it had gone.

To say that I could have wept is ridiculous. I *did* weep. I did just have enough money to go and buy another but that was the end of my savings. It would leave me with nothing for the hungry, let alone the rainy, day. Naturally I went back to the store and got another one and so it was that for the first time ever I turned up at an athletics meeting wearing something other than a school or college uniform. It was a beautiful moment, but it would be untrue to claim that we had yet quite arrived.

By 'we' I mean Bridget Robinson and myself, the novices of the team. From start to finish we never really understood what the whole expensive expedition was about. We didn't train very much and we certainly didn't train every day. It never occurred to us that that was what one was expected to do. All we knew was that we were there because we had a certain natural talent and we were there on merit, if the definition of that was that there wasn't anyone better around in our country. We were there for a super, exciting holiday among lots of famous people, and when it came to the athletics we would do our absolute utmost and not become bitter and twisted hulks of humanity when we lost. In the meantime there were far more fundamental matters to contend with, such as inadvertently packing our white berets in our main advance luggage so that we shouldn't have to wear them on the journey to Cardiff. We both detested hats and we really worked hard on the scheme to lose them. We loved our white kid leather Van Dal shoes and we knew we'd really arrived in the International Set when some of the boxers took us down to Barry Island one night and gave us a super time on the dodgems and the Big Dipper and we all finished up dining on candy floss which I'd never eaten before.

We shared a billet in a bottle-green Nissen hut on an RAF station. It had two beds and a locker in which we could hang our clothes, in my case little more than my official uniform, my doubly-precious grey skirt and the only track suit I possessed. Today's international athlete may have found it somewhat monastic but since I didn't know the difference between Sparta and the Savoy at the time I was deliriously happy. It is only since that I've learned that sophistication can be an unsettling thing. As for food, I'd never seen anything like it. Dinner in my first digs in Belfast had comprised, on a good night, two slices of spam, one tomato and some bread and butter. Here there were sizzling chops for lunch and delicious steak for dinner followed by super puddings immersed in fresh cream.

I cried at the opening ceremony because it was all so moving and beautiful and I, Mary Elizabeth Peters, who was hopeless at Latin, was there in my own right in the presence of the Queen. Then the Games got underway and I found myself caught up in this whirl-wind of movement. There were no seniors or juniors, no VIPs and also-rans. I was staggered to discover that you could queue up in the restaurant just behind, or just in front of, yesterday's gold medallist whose photograph was in every newspaper. He took his turn with the rest. If I'd known what democracy meant I would have decided that this was it. I even met the great sprint champion Mike Agostini, possibly the most glamourous figure at the entire Games. Sixteen years later I ran into Mike again at the Common-wealth Games in New Zealand. 'Christ,' he said, 'I remember meet-ing you in Cardiff. You know, in those days I used to think the great thing in life was to go around and screw everybody. Nowadays I've got a gorgeous wife and gorgeous kids and some gorgeous girl could come along here now and I wouldn't even be interested.' I liked Agostini then and I think I like him now even more.

At some point the ceremonial and the eating and the chat had to stop and we had to get down to the Games. In those days there was no pentathlon. I was in for the shot and the high jump and, as reluctantly as at least three other members of the Northern Ireland women's team, the relay.

Well, you've got to start somewhere, and as soon as I went out to the high jump area I had the first taste of what the big league was all about. The bar was resting at 4 ft 10 in and no one had taken her track suit off yet. Four ft 10 in was within a fraction of the best I'd ever achieved. We warmed up and stripped down. The stars left their conversation, hopped over and came back to pick up the sentence they'd broken off a moment ago. I concentrated like hell, ran like fury and got over. Jubilation. Ecstasy. Then they moved it up to 5 ft and that was me, out of the high jump. So we came to the shot. By my own standards I didn't do badly at all and I would like to point out that I didn't finish up last in the Commonwealth. Nine took part and although I don't recall now the lady's name or which country she came from, one of them actually finished behind me.

There remained the dreaded relay which some economy-minded chauvinist had decided we must enter. Of the four of us only Maeve Kyle was a specialist sprinter. Thelma was the high jump queen, Bridget threw the javelin and I, as we've established, enjoyed candy floss. But we had to face it so we went out for our heat knowing that our only reward could be a humiliating beating. So it was. We were last by miles. But that wasn't quite the end of it. We were discreetly walking away when we were informed that one of the teams had been disqualified over a baton change. As there had been only four teams in our heat in the first place we would be overjoyed to know, said our happy informant, that Northern Ireland's women had qualified for the final.

I repeat, it was four gliders trying to stop the Luftwaffe. It was four windjammers in pursuit of the Sixth Fleet. There is a photograph somewhere showing me handing over the baton at the end of the third leg to Maeve Kyle. If you ever see it note the classical style. Note, also, on the right-hand end of the picture, that the winners, at that precise moment, were breaking the tape. They'd broken the world record, that's all.

Cardiff staged the most marvellous Games and every moment was a joy. That I came away enriched as a person but still athletically naive may not be as culpable as it sounds. Of course, my approach had been too matter-of-fact, but it occurs to me, knowing what I now know about the demands on the modern athlete, whether we haven't come too far? When victory is the result of obsession rather than dedication, when training demands submission rather than sacrifice, I am inclined to think we might have lost sight of our values. In my own case I was a free agent and chose to go along with the devouring system but more recently I have been in contact with children, literally one third of the age I was when I competed at Cardiff, who appear to have no choice in the matter.

On my way home from the New Zealand Commonwealth Games in 1974 I called in at Sydney and was staying there with my brother when I received an invitation to attend a meeting of the New South Wales Little Athletes, aged six to twelve. It wasn't what the kids were doing which horrified me. It was the obvious, maniac ambition of their parents which made me feel quite ill.

Watching their faces I could see a ruthlessness and determination to make certain their children emerge as winners, regardless of cost. Perhaps, in some cases, it was to compensate for their own anonymity in an adult world. But I knew as I watched that the adrenalin there was flowing in the spectators, not the tiny competitors. The aggression was between parent and parent, not runner and runner, and I had a good idea that some of those kids were going to get hell when they got home if they hadn't come up to expectation. Young Australian swimmers, of course, train under a still more severe regime, getting up in the middle of the night to start training, then going to school, then returning to the pool as soon as lessons are over.

I know, in a small way, what parental ambitions can do to a child later in life. My father was, and remained, ambitious for me and I know that over a number of years it did not improve our relationship. What I saw at that Australian trackside was that same syndrome multiplied a hundred times. I think it would have been a marvellous system had that kind of sustained training and competition started at the age of eleven instead of six. It may, as it is, yield an extra gold medal at an Olympic Games eight, twelve or sixteen years from now, but it could just break a few hundred lives in the process. I concluded you have to be a small nation with a large complex of some kind to indulge in that kind of production-line madness. I expressed this opinion to one or two local officials of the scheme and felt they didn't necessarily appreciate it.

It didn't matter much. For one thing I would have banned those parents to a point out of harm's way the moment they opened their mouths to scream for their offspring. And for another I had been quite amused at a small incident which occurred when I arrived. 'And here,' said a sort of disc-jockey voice over the public address, 'is Miss Mary Peters who's just been to the Commonwealth Games and won a gold for Australia.'

Ah well, I thought, you can't win 'em for everybody. If the idiot can't even recognise his own heroes (and Australia had just won the Games and twenty-nine golds without any help from Northern Ireland at all) maybe he is ideally suited to his present position of drill-sergeant to the infants' class.

Cardiff, for me in 1958, was absurdly different. I went there without any predetermined targets and came away without any overwhelming sense of failure. I'd just been to the Commonwealth Games, that's all. Today there would probably be a national inquiry into the reasons for my failure. That would be wrong. I don't decry any youngster being sent to one of the big ones just to get the feel of the atmosphere and get used to rubbing shoulders with the big names and knowing what you have to do to get lunch or the laundry or a letter posted. That's experience, and if you're planning to stay around for a year or two that's something you can't pick up by correspondence course.

Back in Belfast I quit the digs with spam on the menu and nowhere to hang your washing and strict orders never to use the telephone. I went instead to live with Granny Murray and her daughter, Helen, who welcomed me as one of the family. They were God-fearing and very kind. I had another two years at the Belfast College of Domestic Science where there were sixteen girls on our course of whom fifteen were better than me at chemistry. My chemistry was so bad that it made my relay running look good. My only hope was to try and memorise it, parrot-wise, and hope that I could understand what the examination questions were even about. I was quite good, though, on the practical side and, in the end, all sixteen of us got through. I'd never really been in two minds about what to do as a career. I could have earned more money, perhaps, in hotel management, but I wanted to be with young people and teaching was the obvious answer. My first job was at Graymount Girls' Secondary School. I spent four years there and it proved to be my last teaching job as well. During that time a short, dark-haired man entered my life.

4. Buster McShane

According to the Oxford Dictionary a coach is a tutor or a trainer: one who gives hints to, or primes others with facts. In the academic world this is probably an adequate definition. In the world of athletics it understates the reality. The relationship between coach and subject is frequently of far deeper psychological complexity than that between the two partners of an average marriage. It can involve something close to a mind-transplant: less the dominance of a weaker will by a stronger one than the actual transference of wills to produce, under extreme pressure, the super-human performance. It is why all the good coaches, at some time or other in their careers, are described on the sports pages as Svengalis. It is journalistic shorthand for a depth of understanding between coach and athlete that is somewhere between the telepathic and the mystical. Mary Peters' Svengali was born Robert Terence McShane. But he always liked to be known by his nickname which was Buster. In fact he never knew whether the 'Terence' should be spelled with one 'r' or two.

I knew very little about Buster McShane when I first saw him except he was a weight-lifting coach to the Northern Ireland team. We had assembled in Belfast to have a group photograph taken before leaving for the Commonwealth Games of 1958. Someone said 'That's Buster McShane' and I saw this rather funny looking little man who seemed to be wearing all the wrong clothes. He had a habit of wearing jackets with enormously broad shoulders, trousers that tended to be so short that you could see the ankle bones above his shoes, and ties that had horizontal and not diagonal stripes. These he would tie in large Windsor knots, which were hardly part of the Belfast sartorial scene at the time. He also had the rather lengthy sideburns which were to become quite fashionable all over the British Isles something like twenty-five years later. Buster had the virtue of not remotely caring what anyone thought of him or his style. He was a happy, amusing man who always seemed to be the centre of groups of people who were laughing. He was eight years older than me and our paths hardly crossed at all during the Games in Cardiff. It was only when I returned to Belfast that, like every other international athlete in the city, I received a letter from him saying that he was starting weight-lifting courses for anyone who would like to attend them. I was very pleased to get his letter. Quite a few of us turned up the first week, half returned the following week and eventually we were whittled down to a hard core of about four. I loved weight-training from the very start. His gym, on the third floor above a pub and a small sewing factory, was a pretty tatty place with holes in the window panes and broken floorboards but it was a vibrant place, full of Buster's enthusiasm. His motto seemed to be dedication with fun. I was still very much a junior international but we had an immediate rapport. I couldn't wait to get out of college to go there in the evenings and was often the first to arrive. That meant collecting the key from Desano's ice cream shop across the road and creeping up to the third floor without the luxury of any lights on the stairs. Then Buster would arrive. He always had a pale complexion and his hair would be sleeked back from his forehead. Somehow there was something quite teddy boyish about his appearance but that never lessened my respect for him. As I got to know him I was able to piece together the background of a quite remarkable man little knowing, of course, that eventually he was to dominate my own career and life.

His iron will had been forged by literally smashing his way out of an underprivileged background. He was born in Canada of Irish parents but then returned to Belfast, a city with which he always had an intense love-hate relationship, to be brought up by his mother and grandmother after his parents' marriage broke up. It was breadline living with no extras or bathrooms. When he left school at fourteen and went to work in the shipyards he was still wearing short trousers. It was there he learned to take no notice of being a mild figure of fun. He was, in fact, almost the prototype seven stone weakling who suddenly saw the advertisement inviting him to stop having the sand kicked into his face. Only in his case it wasn't an advertisement: it was a book in Smithfield's, the secondhand booksellers, about bodybuilding and physical education. Buster bought it on the never-never and went away to change his life.

Weights were prohibitively expensive so he made some from metal he stole from the shipyards. The only way he could fool the security check at the gates was to tie the weights to a piece of rope, put the rope round his neck and then slip the weights into his pockets or down his trouser legs. His legs would be bruised and his neck would be chaffed but his collection of body-building equipment back in his bedroom soon became so impressive that his grandmother lived in constant fear of the whole lot crashing through the floor into the kitchen. His next ambition was to own a set of chest-expanders he had seen in a shop window. They were far beyond the reach of his purse but the shopkeeper was so struck by Buster's almost paranoic determination to build up his tiny frame that he said: 'If you can pull them out fully you can have them for nothing.' It was a challenge that Buster couldn't refuse. He borrowed another set of expanders from a friend, took them home and almost burst his lungs learning how to master them. Eventually he went back to the shop like some miniature champion bending down to pick up the gauntlet. The shopkeeper gathered his entire staff together to witness the test. Buster gripped the handles, took a huge breath and stretched the expanders right across his chest. The owner kept his part of the bargain and Buster's growing armoury over the kitchen had increased by another few pounds.

He exercised his brain just as much as his body. He was a voracious reader of everything, but particularly medical, physical education and mechanical magazines. He also wrote articles for weight-lifting and physical culture papers, even though his spelling at that stage was suffering from the fact that he had had to leave school to go and earn his keep as soon as the law permitted. His grandmother used to recall how Buster would be sitting at the kitchen table and continually shouting to her in the yard: 'Granny, how do you spell so-and-so?' She used to rush into the house to reprimand him. 'Don't shout out things like that, son. The neighbours will think you're stupid.' She was ambitious for him, too, and used to worship him. It was typical of Buster that he never totally mastered spelling. His brain and thoughts were always flashing way ahead of the word he was writing and, anyway, he didn't see much merit in mastering what he only regarded as the logistical matter of getting the letters in the right order. Life was about much more than that. He used to draw, as well, and became a very talented cartoonist. For a while the *Daily Mirror* used some of his cartoons in Ireland. They were mostly political, rarely about sport. It was almost inevitable, with his background in the climate of the times, that he should have been extremely left-wing for a while. He drifted away from Marxism as he grew older and I don't think he ever became associated with any political movement. He was such an original thinker that he was a one-man party in himself.

There is no doubt that his enormous self-confidence as an adult came directly from his decision to take up body-building. He was self-made in every sense of the phrase. When he had any extra money to spare he would buy himself an extra egg so that he could have two instead of one for a meal, which the family budget couldn't run to. He was very conscious that he needed the protein to build up his body and the life he led as a teenager burned up calories at a fearful rate. Work started early in the shipyards and as soon as his shift was done there he would rush home and get to a gym for weight-training every night. At one period, after getting soaked by rain rushing between his work and his passion, he contracted pneumonia. It didn't deter him. Nothing deterred him. He became an international weightlifter, a weight-lifting coach, a famous figure in the body-building field, one of the best-developed men in that highly competitive business, a man respected throughout the world in the field of physical education, a successful businessman and the owner of an extremely cultivated mind who thought freely and lived a packed life with style.

His early days of extreme left-wing thinking and fiercely militant trades-unionism may seem incompatible with his later life, when he loved to acquire good paintings and drive fast, expensive cars. But it wasn't. He enjoyed his success and liked to be seen to be successful but he never forgot those early days or renounced his principles of humanitarianism.

His name, McShane, would have implied to most people in Northern Ireland that he was a Catholic, but he wasn't. There were even those who thought the nickname 'Buster' was a kind of smokescreen for Christian names like Seamus or Patrick which would have labelled him, beyond all bigots' doubts, as a follower of Rome. But he was hiding nothing. He was christened Robert

Terence and was promptly rechristened 'Buster' by his family as
soon as he was old enough to totter around. Apparently he was both
boisterous and clumsy and he had a terrible record of breaking
everything from crockery to small but treasured family heirlooms.
Buster he became, and Buster he remained to his mother, his
grandmother, all his friends and, later, his wife. I never called him
anything else.

In fact he was brought up as a Protestant and was sent to church
regularly and took part in a lot of church activities. His talent for
art was soon recruited to provide a new set of hymn numbers to be
slipped into the frame each Sunday. But if they thought they were
training a God-fearing sidesman, or even a lay preacher, of the
future, they must have been sorely disappointed. Buster questioned
everything from the immaculate conception to the resurrection and
came to the conclusion that neither made as much sense to him as
the theory of evolution. Nor did he think that the religious differences between people who regularly worshipped the same God had
done a great deal for the happiness of Northern Ireland. He became
an atheist and remained one.

He was never discourteous to people of deep religious faith but he
could be quite violent in his scorn of those who tried to impose
their views from a platform of piety. I recall waiting in his car for
him one Saturday morning in Belfast when he went into a store to
collect the inevitable armful of books and magazines for his weekend
reading. On the street corner, wearing a placard bearing some such
suggestion as 'The Wages of Sin is Death,' a self-elected saver of
souls was hammering out his message to all the passing sinners out
buying things like bacon, Persil or a new pair of shoes. Buster
glanced at him on his way back, got into the car and slammed the
door in temper. 'Just look at that stupid bastard standing there –
preaching. Why doesn't the fool get out and *do* something. Who's
he influencing? No one.' He could never understand why a person
could be demonstrative and ineffectual at the same time.

His faith, like his politics, was utterly practical. He was an
enormously out-going person who did not shy away from other
people's problems. Nor did his success insulate him from those
who had failed to fight their way out of the back streets. A casual
meeting with a complete stranger at an auction sale, for example,
was the start of something quite big. The man was looking for a

cheap typewriter and filing cabinet to help a small organisation known somewhat prosaically as the 'Old People's Coal and Grocery Fund.' Buster gave him a few shillings towards them and then started asking questions. For years after that every penny we collected at our talks and demonstrations about physical fitness went to that fund. Buster also started visiting old people all over the city and on both sides of the sectarian line. Quite often, a few days after his visits, a blanket or some other small comfort would arrive. Around Christmas the fund would send out something like 150 hampers to needy cases and Buster would comb through the list of gifts with a very critical eye. 'A bottle of lemonade isn't very nutritious,' he would say, and insist the committee changed it for a tin of condensed milk. He would have been mortified if there had ever been any publicity about this side of his nature. He was quite content to be known as a rebel. When the BBC produced their excellent television documentary on his life and work in Northern Ireland he must have shocked many people by saying in it, 'I gave up religion at sixteen. I thought it was an unhealthy thing.' Buster, above all, wasn't a hypocrite.

I, too, am an atheist. You may well suspect that that is because of Buster's influence, but that is not so. His outlook really only confirmed views that had been growing in me for a long time. They started, naïvely, with my mother's death when I was consumed by a bitterness that all the ministers who visited could do nothing for her. Those are no grounds to reject a faith but, as I grew older in a country where religion often conceals bigotry of the worse kind, I could only come to the conclusion that the loving God for whom they dressed up in their best clothes every Sunday did not exist. It was a considerable rejection because I, too, had been brought up according to a fairly strict Christian code. As Northern Ireland people will recognise, from the school I went to, it was the Protestant code. Later, in lodgings in Belfast, I came under the influence of a Presbyterian family whose attitudes to the Sabbath were so strict and rigid that to file your nails or clean your shoes on a Sunday were sins to be condemned in the same breath as cruelty or culpable homicide. Out of respect for their habits I went to church regularly for almost two years. During that time I was rarely spoken to by another parishioner unless they were to say 'Good morning' in reply to my 'Good morning.' I could not sing and nor could I understand the value of sermons which were either academic or abstract to a city whose people needed love and humanity to be preached in the simplest terms. It was in the pews of that church that I became an atheist with no help from Buster McShane at all.

My outlook may change, but I doubt it. I am happy to say that in the years that followed, as we became quite well known in Belfast, Buster and I were made as welcome in the Protestant Shankill Road as in the Catholic Falls. If we were invited to speak in one we made sure we received an invitation to speak in the other. That the same options are not open to everyone only illustrates the great sadness of the division that separates our city. I have never previously spoken or written about my attitudes to religion, since they are probably more personal than profound. But it may help to explain my answers to those many people over the years who have asked me to attend sportsmen's services or read the lesson in churches. I have always said no. I try to help young or old people in other ways. In any way that can help to unite our community.

In those early years in Belfast, however, Buster and I had far more personal motives and ambitions. Mine was to develop into a good athlete, Buster's to develop his business from a makeshift third-floor gymnasium into a health club. It was perhaps inevitable that we were on the kind of collision course that was to lead to him suggesting that he should become my full-time coach. For eighteen months I had merely been one of the athletes using his weight-lifting equipment and accommodation. Now as he was planning to move to new premises – once again on a top floor but this time at least with some wallpaper and a changing room boasting the ultimate luxury of a mirror – he told me that he thought I was not getting the best out of my shot-putting with the strength I was developing. Could he become my coach? I did not hesitate to say yes. He had this quite extraordinary ability to give you a surging confidence.

Our first session as athlete and coach was on a damp day in the depths of winter in Ormeau Park. The very first time I put the shot under his direction it hit the ground with a splosh and almost disappeared like a cannonball sinking into a rice pudding. Buster did not bat an eyelid. He removed a large, immaculate white handkerchief from his pocket, prised the shot out of the turf, carefully wiped it perfectly clean and handed it back to me for the next throw. Like all great coaches he could be an extreme bully, but when bullying was unnecessary he could display the kind of gallantry which is normally associated with those of no less than one thousand years of Spanish ancestry.

The following year, after the Commonwealth Games in Perth, he invited me to join the business. My role was clearly defined from the start. I was to be the dog's-body factotum around the latest gym he had taken, this time in Upper Church Lane, Belfast, and this time with real class. It had lino on the floor. It was to be a part-time appointment which I could work in with my teaching job. Its first attraction was that I would no longer have to pay my weekly subscription which had now risen to fifty pence a week. I was still thinking about this when Buster made up my mind for me by tearing up my membership card. I did some filing, some general office work and some health instruction in the gymnasium. As far as I was concerned this may have been of some small benefit to overweight businessmen directly in line for heart-attacks and housewives who just wanted to keep in trim so that they would be more attractive to their husbands and far better-tempered with their children at home. I do not regard this as a particularly degrading or sinful occupation but, of course, I was now, under the quite ludicrous law laid down by the millionaires and noblemen of the International Olympic Committee, a professional. Within their terms of reference I was a cheat throughout the remainder of my athletic career. By their definition I was a perjurer every time I stood there at subsequent Olympic Games and allowed the oath of amateurism to be taken solemnly in my name. I was 'investigated' several times and on each occasion had no compunction at all about telling the first lie that came into my head. Of course I wasn't a professional. I was spending more out of my teaching salary of nine pounds a week on athletics than I could ever afford. Proportionately I was spending more to represent my country at sport than Mr Avery Brundage was spending on his renowned collection of Chinese jade which, ultimately, was valued at thirty-five million pounds. I never had a penny to spare because I was spending it all on sport. Anyway, the anomalies of the definition of amateurism were so huge that had I been undertaking the same sports instruction in a school or in the armed forces I would have been regarded as a true-blue amateur, because that's what the rule book said. When the rules are foolish you are entitled to ignore them. This, by the way, is not what certain newspapers like to regard as a 'sensational revelation'. There is nothing sensational about it at all and nor am I revealing anything which anyone remotely connected with athletics hasn't known for years. If you wanted to make money in the late 1950's or early 1960's the last thing you became was a churchmouse or an Olympic competitor.

The situation didn't change when Buster invited me to join his staff full-time. I was now being offered precisely the career that both my father and my headmaster wanted for me when I came to leave school. I hesitated because I was enjoying teaching domestic science and I was quite good at it. But, as I improved as an athlete, certain other pressures were growing. I had the chance to go abroad on more and more overseas trips and while my headmistress could not have been kinder or more co-operative, the Ministry of Education were proving somewhat difficult. They were prepared to allow me leave of absence but without pay. I took their point but there was the small problem of how I was going to eat or pay the rent. Buster's usual pragmatism settled my dilemma. 'Come and join me,' he said, 'and the problem won't be there any more.' I went and joined Buster.

They were days of supreme happiness. The gymnasium was becoming well known in the city and more and more people were enrolling to take off weight, put on weight or just redistribute their weight to the places where it looked a little more flattering. As the clientele grew so did the staff. I finished up in a team of four instructresses who were living proof that women can work together happily. There was Irene Miskimmon who could have walked off with the Miss Ireland title any time she wanted, only she was too modest to go in for it. There was Hilary Rush, who was smaller and had an enormous sense of fun. And there was wee Jean Mitchell who never forgot to bring the cheroots along when we had saved up enough money to get ourselves dolled up and go out on the town for a night together. We worked increasingly long hours, sometimes from ten in the morning until nine in the evening, and I think I write the truth when I claim that in our years together we never had a cross word. Nor were there any more slightly resentful looks when I went away on my athletic trips. They were always happy for me to go and were delighted when I did well.

Altogether we had nine years in that gym. Eventually the lino gave way to carpets and sauna baths were built in, but it never lost its homely atmosphere. The only small panic I remember there was when the floor below us fell vacant and was taken over by a gentleman who insisted in transforming it into a strip club. This might have been very good for his bank balance but it didn't augur too well for ours. Many of our clients were eminently respectable and Buster reasoned that they wouldn't be too happy about being seen going in and out of a doorway which was now being frequented by rather unhappy looking men in traditionally dirty raincoats. He tried to get an injunction against the club but failed.

There is a sadly ironic end to the story. We finally moved out to go into palatial new premises in Upper Arthur Street. On a Sunday evening three months later the old building was bombed out of existence. I went down to look at it the following morning and stood rather tearfully on the far pavement, remembering the happy times we had had there. The roof was blasted away and the floor of our gym was sagging down at forty-five degrees. We had left a little equipment there as a precaution against our new building being the target for a bomb attack. It was strewn around everywhere and the vibrator belts were hanging down like ladies' garters which had been abandoned in a hurry.

A lady beside me on the pavement said, 'Isn't it desperate.' I was still sniffing a little and I said, 'Yes . . . and I used to work there.' The lady looked me up and down with what appeared to be surprise. 'There now,' she said, 'I didn't even know we'd ever had a strip club in Belfast.'

The dominating figure of all these years was Buster. It is inevitable that his name will recur again and again in this story so it is perhaps important that I do not eulogise or paint a picture of a paragon. He had enormous magnetism and infectious enthusiasm but modesty did not bother him overmuch and he could certainly be less than gentle on occasions.

Once, coming home from Australia, we were forced by fog to spend a couple of days in Calcutta. Although it was long after Partition some of the old habits of the Raj still survived. We were booked into an old colonial-style hotel and Buster saw red every time he heard some elderly patron clicking his fingers and then saw half a dozen little Indian waiters tumbling over one another to answer the master's call. He was always the champion of the under-privileged though we were soon to realise that the waiters were the lucky ones. It was impossible to walk through the streets at night without picking your way carefully through thousands of people huddled up in blankets or sheets on the pavements. I hated the place.

It was at about this time that Buster had started his art collection and it was now as impossible for him to pass an art gallery as it always had been for him to pass a bookshop. In one gallery in Calcutta he saw a picture of a man reading a newspaper at a pavement café. To me it was just another picture but he recognised the value of it immediately and this was confirmed when he turned it over and discovered the name of an artist who had recently won an important Italian award. At forty pounds, it was one of the few genuine bargains still to be picked up in the Orient. Naturally he did not have anything as practical as money on him so I had to go and cash some of my travellers' cheques and raise it for him. He went back and bought it. What fascinated me, even though I knew him well by then, was that he refused to let them wrap it. It was large and valuable and awkward to carry through customs and on to airplanes but Buster was determined that everyone should see him as a connoisseur and a good judge of art. It was the exhibitionist streak which he never lost. He carried it through the streets of Calcutta. He carried it off the plane in London in such a gale that when the wind got under it he was almost lifted off his feet. But people around him were almost walking upside down to see what masterpiece he had bought and that Buster loved.

That painting was almost the first really good piece he had in his collection and is now extremely valuable. Continually he was encouraging me to buy something of real value like that but I've never had any real appreciation of art and I always had the nagging thought that I was going to be cheated. Buster, meanwhile, was having to move house to find room for everything he was beginning to accumulate. He first built himself a bungalow, with lots of unusual brickwork, based on the then startlingly contemporary styles of the Commonwealth Village in Perth. Later he moved to a large, beautiful house in the suburbs of Belfast. It was there that the photograph on the dust-jacket of this book was taken. The wall is Buster's back wall and the view is the view to which Buster woke every morning.

He was always rightly proud that it was a small contrast to the house without a bathroom and the shipyards under early morning mist.

When he came finally to build his ultimate dream of a health club it was, once more, completely his personal design. All the architect had to do was make the ideas professionally viable. Buster knew that the most advanced health clubs were in America so that was where we went, after the Tokyo Olympics. We must have visited between fifty and sixty traipsing by way of Honolulu to Los Angeles and San Francisco and Washington and New York. Buster went into every one of them as though it were the Taj Mahal all over again, looking, peering, asking questions. Some of them were exclusively for women and he would be refused admittance. That was where I came in. I would be packed off to bring back a full report. I was still very reticent about that kind of business and I was always in danger of falling victim to paying a full year's subscription before I could get out again. I became absolutely fed up with it but Buster hammered his way onward, bursting through doors and demanding to know everything. The result was that, at the end of that trip, there was probably no man living who knew more about modern gymnasia. He was also subtly teaching me the business along the way. He never got tired. He was living confirmation that good health heightens the enjoyment of everything in life.

In everything he did he set his sights high. He could be hard on himself and those around him in times of failure. Just occasionally his quick, explosive temper showed through and though the following incident happened quite late in my athletic career this, perhaps, is the place to record it.

We were preparing for the big one, the Munich Olympics of 1972, and all was not going well. I had been pestered with achilles tendon trouble and was getting pain every time I ran. The days were running out and our nerve-ends were beginning to show. It just wasn't going the way we had planned.

One afternoon, out at the Queen's University track, I was putting the shot incredibly badly and with each successive throw was becoming more tense. 'I don't know what the hell you're doing,' snapped Buster, 'but you're certainly not doing it right.' That was all I needed. I thumped the shot down on the gravel and snapped back, 'Well, you're my coach. *You* tell *me* what I'm doing wrong.'

The next thing I knew I was lying flat on the ground. Buster had hit me. He struck me so hard that he knocked me clean off my feet and I lay there shocked and bewildered and desperately hurt, not from physical pain but because of what had happened between us. We were both acting totally out of character. For me to retaliate, for him to hit me were things that just didn't happen between us.

I got to my feet, but I was so angry I couldn't talk to him. I walked away, right down to the far end of the track. There are few athletic grounds in the world with more beautiful surroundings than that of Queen's University but I saw nothing. Only red. Eventually I turned and went back, noticing thankfully on the way that at least there were no witnesses to what had just happened. News of incidents like that spread like a bush-fire.

When I reached Buster he started to laugh. 'How the hell did you get down there on the track?' he said. 'Because you knocked me there,' I said. 'My father never even did a thing like that to me and you'll never do it again.' We finished the training session and went to the car. Buster suggested we had lunch somewhere. 'Take me home,' I said, and we drove in silence across the city. He pulled in to the kerb and I got out, slammed the door and ran into my flat, determined to take no telephone calls. I just had to sort out in my own mind whether I was going to continue in athletics or not. I knew that if I were to break with Buster I would get out of sport altogether. I would never work under another coach.

The telephone rang. I sat there and stared at it but it went on ringing. Whoever it was knew I was in and the only person who could know that was Buster McShane. I knew that it was only his desire for me to do well that had made him do that awful thing. But did mere ambition justify people treating one another like brutal sub-humans? The telephone continued to ring.

I walked across and picked up the receiver. Buster's voice said, 'I'm sorry, P, I shouldn't have done it.' It was the only time he ever apologised to me in his life.

5. *Queen of the Workers*

On a blistering summer afternoon in 1961, in the Spanish resort of Tossa-de-Mar, there appeared a bizarre figure whose apparel suggested she was a fugitive from St Trinian's on her way to a Co-op staff dance or, alternatively, vice versa. She wore a green blazer, a home-made cocktail-length dress of pink crêpe, a pair of stiletto-heeled, winkle-picker shoes which were visibly killing her, and swayed with exhaustion beneath the weight of an enormous suitcase. Tossa-de-Mar, then the Acapulco of the package holiday circuit, neither batted an eyelid nor offered her a hand. It was no way to treat a young lady who had just become Britain's newest athletics star.

What was I to do? For months Joan Wallace and I had saved for this holiday-of-a-lifetime on the Costa Brava. We'd been students together and now we were both teachers in Belfast and on the money that pays you don't just chuck it all overboard because you receive a letter inviting you to represent Great Britain in an athletics match against Hungary at the White City, London. I was dying for the invitation but I was paying for the holiday and fate decreed that both things would happen on the same day. Had I known Buster then as I was to know him later he would have gone to the telephone, sorted it out in thirty seconds and told me what to do. Instead of which I was staying with my family in Lancashire and listening to my father's advice. 'There's nothing for it,' he said, 'you'll just have to decide between one or the other.' That settled it. I was determined to do both. Even now the cheek of what I did makes me go cold. I went to a phone box and contacted Jack Crump, secretary of the British Amateur Athletic Board. It was the nearest I had yet been to direct contact with God. 'Mr Crump,' I began, stumbling about to explain my predicament, 'I've got this invitation to compete at the White City but I've got this holiday booked in . . .' Mr Crump cut me off very gently and explained that of course there was no complication at all. My friends simply went on ahead to Spain, I competed in London and flew out on a later plane to join them. Naturally my one-way ticket to Spain would be paid for by the Athletic Board who were almost unreasonably detaining me in London for their own benefit. Would I please have a very successful athletics meeting and a very happy holiday?

I had never heard anything like it. This was star treatment. It appeared that I had arrived.

This was my first United Kingdom international selection and there was no doubt who was responsible for it. Marea Hartman, the England women's team manager, had invited me to join her own club, the Spartan Ladies Athletic Club of London, and performing for them at Hurlingham I had suddenly pulled out a shot-put of something like 39 ft 11 in. This was almost as good as anything achieved by the two best shot-putters in the country. Clearly I was now earmarked as someone to encourage and so, after the two comparatively quiet summers since the Cardiff Commonwealth Games, I was on the way. I performed quite well against Hungary but it must say something about my temperament that I was equally excited about the prospect of going on holiday to Spain that same evening.

I have travelled many thousands of miles all over the world since then but I don't think I have ever had a more adventurous journey. I was the classic innocent abroad. I went to London Airport straight from a reception in Park Lane and took my seat in the plane next to a very smooth looking gentleman who insisted that there was absolutely nothing to this flying business at all. 'Just sit back there, relax and enjoy it,' he said. Unfortunately our plane passed through an area of mild turbulance which caused my companion to lose his composure for a moment or two while he was quite spectacularly ill all over the place. We arrived in Barcelona about two o'clock the following morning. The first thing I discovered was that the courier who was going to meet me hadn't turned up. The second thing was that my luggage had been left behind in London. The third was that I had not the faintest idea how far away Tossa was or even in which direction it lay. The fourth was that I had no cash, only travellers' cheques, and none of the airport banks was open.

The fifth was that I desperately wanted to visit the loo, but I'd been informed that all Spanish lavatories are custom-built to accommodate men and women simultaneously. They weren't getting me into one of those. So I sat there all night, shifting uneasily through a number of yoga positions, while they washed the floor under my feet.

Finally help arrived in the form of the next flight in from London. My luggage was on it, a courier was present and eventually they squeezed me into a taxi with three men who were also bound for the Costa Brava. Happily their physiological needs soon happened to coincide with my own. They stopped the taxi and must have been astonished to see Britain's newest international athlete break a world record to beat them to the toilet. By not much later than three o'clock that afternoon I was standing, in all my Park Lane finery, in High Street, Tossa. I staggered to the hotel, joined my friends, flopped out on the beach in the blazing sun and passed out like a light. Naturally I would have burned to a frazzle had someone not taken mercy and covered my tender white body with beach towels. 'Mary P,' I vowed when I woke up, 'if you're going to conquer anything you're going to have to start getting organised. What's more, if you can make an international team as a shot-putter, just think what you could do if you really got down to strict training.' It was probably the first time I ever realised my own potential.

Even so, the resolution to 'get organised' was easier said than achieved. Later that summer we went on to the Continent again for matches against Germany and Poland. Now the completely haphazard approach I had taken to the Cardiff Games was gone. I *wanted* a disciplined existence, I *wanted* to dedicate myself to the business of winning, yet all I found was confusion. One afternoon I was getting down to some hard practice on a training ground when, one by one, almost every member of the male English 'heavy mob' came by to have a look at my method. One said that I was doing this wrong, another said I was doing that wrong, almost no one suggested I was doing anything right at all. 'If I'm *that* bloody bad,' I asked myself, 'what on earth am I doing here?' I am sure they all meant well but they certainly didn't do much for my confidence. I went to find a shoulder to weep on and it was lucky that the shoulder belonged to Denis Watts, one of the most gentle and human and understanding men in British athletics. Denis was national coach and, like myself, came from Liverpool. He knew that

I had just begun training under Buster in Belfast but that in no way altered his attitude when confronted by a crestfallen and rather tearful girl who badly needed her shattered ego to be pieced together right there and then. He talked to me a great deal and did much to sort me out at a critical time. Later when I returned to Northern Ireland he continued his confidence-building programme by sending me lots of amusing little notes all designed to impress on me the fact that I had a great future in athletics as long as I could believe in myself. His methods were in direct contrast to Buster's. Occasionally when I was over in Liverpool visiting relatives I would go and train with him at the Liverpool University track. If the day was cold he would bring a hot water bottle to training so that the shot I was to tuck between my cheek and neck would be warmed-up for use. He was, and is, a cuddly, lovable man and I owe him a great deal for pulling me through one of the great depressions of my life. It is trite to say that without believing in yourself you can achieve nothing, but, in my case, it took an agonisingly long time for that simple fact to sink in.

The irony is that as soon as it had another figure was to enter my life to remind me that there are widely contrasting degrees of self-confidence. When I first set eyes on her she was stepping out of a sports car, escorted by a real live Siamese prince and looking as though she was about to pose for one of those glossy advertisements for 150 guinea dresses in *Vogue*. In fact she was arriving to compete in a British Pentathlon Championship, but that was how Mary Toomey – then Mary Bignal, later to be Mary Rand – liked to make her entrances everywhere. She was radiantly beautiful, had enormous style, apparently travelled everywhere with an entourage of admirers, was always surrounded by reporters, knew every top athlete in the world by Christian name and, all in all, gave the impression that Hollywood was wherever she happened to be. I was there with Doris and my father.

I watched her, mesmerised and fascinated, across the restaurant. She laughed a lot, was easy with everyone but, above all, seemed utterly blasé about the stir she was creating. I could think of no greater gulf between the way of life of two human beings than her's and mine. Watching her, knowing that I was shortly to be out there competing against her, almost made me a nervous wreck on the spot. I was back in that street in Tossa wearing all the wrong clothes all over again. She was two years younger than me and, as I was to discover later, came from a very similar social background but at that moment she was virtually everything I wanted to be. I had the feeling, there and then, that I was destined to live in this dazzling girl's shadow for the next few years and so it proved to be. I neither had nor have any resentement about it. She was to become the greatest all-round woman athlete I have ever met and we were to build a deep and lasting friendship before it was all over.

I was to have one brief moment in the spotlight when to everyone's surprise, not the least my own, I went to the European Championships of 1962 and finished fifth, well above my old heroine, Thelma Hopkins. These were only the second major Games in which I had competed and they were the first outside Britain. A fifth place in that highly-competitive field was, by any standards, a good achievement, but to have finished so far ahead of Thelma in a pentathlon really did end the years in which I had played lady-in-waiting to the great star of Northern Ireland. But now I was to play lady-in-waiting to the greatest star in all Britain. It seemed to be my eternal role.

To say that Mary was the leading all-round sportswoman of my generation may imply that I am finding excuses for never having beaten her in a pentathlon. This isn't so. She would have emerged as a star at almost any branch of sport to which she applied her enormous talents. She was a beautiful swimmer and an outstanding hockey player. In South Africa on one occasion we were watching some local ladies give a demonstration on a trampoline. We were both invited to have a go. With some embarrassment I bounced around on it for a few moments and than made way for Mary. Mary's performance could have been televised. It was quite outstanding and I am sure the local ladies didn't believe her when she confessed afterwards that she had only ever been on a trampoline twice previously in her life. On another occasion she was invited to present the awards at one of the *News of the World's* nationwide darts competitions. One of the attractions was a set of gold darts to be presented to the person who threw the first bull. Mary was to set the competition going by throwing the first dart. It was quite typical of her that she took careful aim, threw that first dart straight into the bull and won the prize for herself. More recently in America I stood with her on the side of a tennis court while her second husband was taking tennis lessons from a professional coach. All the while she was watching I could sense her impatience. She was itching to be playing herself. Eventually her chance came and she went on to the court to play as if she had just spent a month warming up with the Wightman Cup Team. The coach merely shook his head and said 'How does she do it?'

It typified her approach to every sport she touched. The secret, I think, was that she was without any kind of embarrassment in any situation. She would have attempted the pole vault had anyone allowed her and she would have done that well, too. In contrast I still get embarrassed, even now and even with just a few close friends, when I try to brush up my swimming or in my efforts to learn to play squash.

In some things I did envy her. I envied the fact that she achieved everything she did without ever having to train as hard as I did. I was never jealous of her easy manner with men but I *was* envious of the number of admirers she had. Everywhere we went there always seemed to be a welcome committee awaiting her with flowers and presents and the promise of parties. She just took it all in her stride, assuming that this was the natural order of things. She had the priceless assets for the athlete of long, slender limbs and even when the competition was at its toughest she remained supremely feminine. In those early days she used to compete with a pearl ring on her engagement finger, rather as though she had just stepped out of a Dior gown to go out on the track. Perhaps she had. I remember one afternoon when she went out and bought ten dresses in a single shopping expedition.

I often wondered where all this supreme assurance and poise came from. She had certainly been adored by her family but she had also gone for a period to Millfield, that remarkable school in Somerset which had produced so many outstanding athletes and sportsmen in the past two decades. She also loved to hold the stage. I said to her once, 'If there was a single chair in a crowded room you would be bloody well sitting on it.' She laughed and denied it, but I was right. In life her liking to be the centre of attraction has not brought her complete happiness but during her phenomenal career in sport it was probably her greatest asset of all. It was a concealed arrogance that made her such a natural leader and supreme competitor.

Above: At the Commonwealth
Games at Cardiff in 1958
with Bridget Robinson the
javelin thrower. We were so
proud of our white Irish
linen outfits and the Van Dal
shoes but hated the little
berets which we tried to
avoid wearing.

Above right: With Thelma
Hopkins who was always so
far ahead of me when I first
took up the pentathlon.

Right: Again at Cardiff with
some of the boxers. I am
wearing the doubly expensive
grey pleated skirt.

Recipe

Take youthful enthusiasm
Add specialised weight training
Tablespoonfuls of coaching
Persevere for six years
Simmering to maturity

Left: When I was teaching at Graymount School I was asked to give my recipe for improvement in sport. On the blackboard are the ingredients for success as I saw them at that time.

Below: At the swimming pool in Tokyo with Pat Pryce and Mary Rand.

Above: This picture shows the enormous amount of food that I consumed every day during 1966 when I needed to build up my weight.

Left: A portrait of Buster taken at home among many of his paintings gathered over the years. It is the Buster we all knew with a glimmer of a smile and a frown. He always liked to set his jaw and I used to tease him that he was trying to look intelligent. The picture above the fireplace was of his Grandmother painted by a local artist.

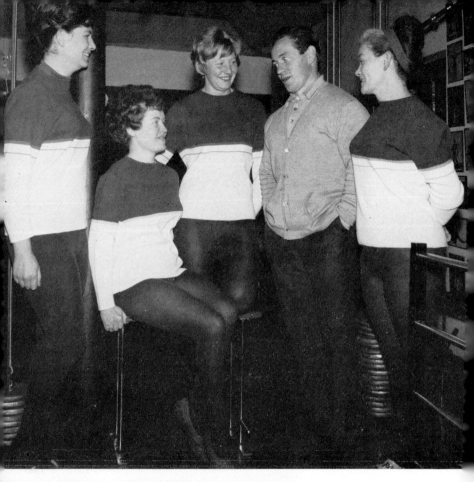

Above: This is an early photograph of the staff at McShane's Health Club. (From left to right) Mrs Margaret McShane, Joan Young, myself, Buster telling us a funny story and wee Jeannie, Buster's cousin.

Left: In Bermuda with Buster and Bill Cook after the Jamaica Commonwealth Games.

It took me a long while to get over those early feelings that she was some kind of goddess among the plebs. They didn't wear off until we were thrown together as both team mates and room mates at the Tokyo Olympics of 1964. There is nothing to beat communal living to learn about a person's real character and I learned much about Mary in those weeks in that room shared by Ann Packer, Pat Pryce, Mary and myself. She was a total fanatic about tidiness and, as the dominant personality in those quarters, she made us live as neat and orderly a life as she did herself. Nothing was permitted to be out of place. To leave a sweater draped over a chair, as I was in the habit of doing, was almost an indictable offence. Everything had to be in its exact place, in our sections of the room as well as hers. Today she is exactly the same about her home life. She would not dream of going out until her home was in perfect order. Nor could she sit in a room, as I have a perhaps reprehensible capacity to do, with magazines strewn about and papers piled up on the table. Everything would have to be neat, in date-order, in logical sequence and squared up with the edge of the table. I have read that Ian Fleming, the writer of the Bond books, had the same obsession. A psychologist would probably find interesting parallels there: they were both immensely successful, charismatic people, envied by millions. But I couldn't help feeling that Mary was making hard work of living. If anything, she was fussy to a fault. But she was a winner and, for her, perfection was no part-time aim.

This was a side of her which the Pressmen who dogged her footsteps and logged her whirlwind romances and travels and marriages didn't see. She was good 'copy' everywhere she went. But she was marvellously human, too. In South Africa we stayed with Jean Ellis and Jean came into our room late one evening to find me shrieking with laughter at the sight of Mary in a long Jane Eyre nightgown. All day long Mary had been enrapturing those rather solid South African gentlemen with skirts so short that nine-tenths of her thighs were exposed for public approval and here she was going to her lonely bed wrapped up like a nun. Maybe it was only reprisal on my part. Our South African tour came just at the time when ultra-short skirts became fashionable, which meant that tights were coming in fast as suspenders were going out. Mary, inevitably, was a leader in the new mode and expressed her horror one morning at the length of the skirt I proposed to wear that day. 'Good God,'

she said, 'you're not going out in *that*. Get it turned up.' We turned
it up to what Mary decreed was the correct length only to discover
that the suspenders to which I had remained resolutely loyal didn't
exactly lend themselves to this kind of experiment. I spent the rest
of the trip wearing Mary's cast-off tights. It was the same with our
hair. Mine, until I grew it, required about as much attention as
Kew Gardens in springtime. I needed perms and curlers and clips
and rollers whereas Mary washed her's every day and just shook it
out and brushed it and looked a million dollars in five minutes flat.
It is hard to see, perhaps, how we became such very close friends,
but we did. The friendship was forged in Tokyo where Mary's
pursuit of the perfection ended with her bringing back to Britain a
complete set of Olympic medals: a gold for her world record leap
in the long-jump, a silver for her second place in the pentathlon and
a bronze for her part in the 4 × 100 metres relay. I was very happy
then to have been some assistance in the pentathlon.

Tokyo, as the current phrase goes, was something else. In fact
that is an apt description because I had never seen anything like it
before and never have since. There were murmurings at the time
that perhaps it was all too early to hold an Olympic Games in a
country which only thirty years before had been waging savage,
imperialist war against the world but I have to be truthful and say
that that thought did not stay with me very long. Tokyo was a
beautiful, thrilling city, a combination of incredible modern bustle
and gentle centuries-old courtesy. One hour you would be sitting
in a taxi being driven at breakneck speeds down an eight-lane city
street or fighting your way into an underground train which looked
as though its destination was to be Wembley on Cup Final day. The
next you would be sitting on cushions in a jeweller's shop where
the business was being transacted as though tomorrow or perhaps
next month would be quite soon enough to conclude a purchase.
I remember going into one where I removed my shoes at the door,
went in and sat down on a cushion on the floor and then went out
again to find that my shoes had been moved around so that they
were pointing towards the exit. It has often intrigued me about how
much a Japanese shoe-turner is paid for an honest week's work.
There were ladies in smart Fifth Avenue clothes and ladies in
kimonos. There were men who looked as though they had been
dressed by some tailor in Savile Row and others who were still

wearing the traditional robes. The schoolchildren, with their glistening black hair and their immaculate white ankle socks, were a picture of health and contentedness. Perhaps this is an over-romantic picture, but I found Tokyo a heavenly place.

This was Asia acting as Olympic host for the first time. A record number of countries, 94, took part and between them sent 5541 competitors. It was also my own first Olympics and I wept with sheer joy at the beautiful opening ceremony. Such emotions wore off, however, when Mary Rand and I came into contact with our leading opponents in the pentathlon. Miss Irina Press and Miss Galina Bystrova, of the Soviet Union, did not exactly welcome us as long-lost or even new friends. In fact if I am forced to say precisely what they looked like to me I have to record that they looked like the full-backs of a soccer team known more for its brutality than its skill. They were undisputed favourites for the gold and silver medals but they recognised in Mary a very dangerous rival. This may well explain their attitude to us which was to treat us with such arrogant condescension that we might well have been a couple of Mayfair debs who had strayed on to the track by mistake.

This was more Mary's problem than mine because she was in there with a chance while it was generally acknowledged that I had none. I hoped for a good placing but little more. For all that, one look at those formidable ladies was enough to make me determined to burst a lung to help Mary in her challenge and it is one of the happiest memories of my life that I was able to do just that.

Mary was in marvellous form throughout those Games, and as we came to the final event of the pentathlon, the 200 metres, she at least had the chance to come between Press, who was certain to take the gold, and Bystrova, who had to run pretty well to take the silver. The draw decreed that while Mary ran against Press in the second heat, I was to run against Bystrova in the first. As a runner Bystrova was something of an unknown quantity, but we knew that if I could beat her then the silver would be Mary's. I ran as I had never run before. Coming down the final straight I thought I would explode but I stayed there and beat her and, despite what you may read in the remaining pages of this book, few races in my life have given me more satisfaction. Mary took the silver medal. That deepened our friendship and it was that day that I lost all awe of her. Athletically we were still not equals but as human beings we rubbed along pretty well, recognising that the other had something to offer. When I was doing the long jump Mary would say 'Why the bloody hell can't you get your bottom up?' When she came into my sphere I would say 'Why the bloody hell don't you learn how to put the shot?' It was the one event of which she had very little idea which just goes to prove, in pentathlon terms, how brilliant she was at everything else.

My final memory of Mary at those Tokyo Games was of her lying in bed in our room the night before her long jump final. She sang a couple of the little songs she used to sing every night to her daughter, Alison. I knew suddenly that she was too tense and nervous to go to sleep and the rest of us joined in until, eventually, we all dropped off. The next day Mary smashed the world record. That's how good she was.

My own placing in the Tokyo pentathlon was fourth, one outside the medal. I was very satisfied. It was as much as Buster thought I could do and better than I thought I could achieve. It was also as much as I would ever achieve while the star of Mary Rand shone so brightly in the firmament. All I could do was work harder and harder. Derek Clarke, for years a leading British decathlete, saw it all. In a letter to me much later he wrote 'Mary Rand was Queen of the Naturals, Mary Peters Queen of the Workers.' The only point was that I hadn't really started working yet.

6. The Runner-Up

In the spring and early summer of 1966 Mary's friends and rivals began to notice a marked change in her physical appearance. Always strongly built, she suddenly broadened rather than blossomed into a massive figure. Some darkly hinted that she had discovered anabolic steroids, the body-building drugs which were pronounced dangerous by sports doctors and declared illegal by all athletics authorities. Some did more than darkly hint. One well known British coach stated categorically that Mary was resorting to steroids to improve her performances. Mary neither sued for slander nor protested. She maintained a complete silence which she breaks here for the first time.

Although the pentathlon was now part of the Olympic programme for women it still hadn't been introduced into the Commonwealth Games. We were back to the old routine. Buster consulted all the charts of comparative performances and decided that I would now concentrate on the shot and go to the 1966 Games in Kingston, Jamaica, with one single target in mind: the gold medal. It was then he announced that to build up strength for this single objective I would undergo a body-building programme which, in theory, sounded unpleasant and which, in practice, proved to be hideously revolting. In short I was to be put on a diet which virtually amounted to forced feeding.

Already I was taking all the vitamin supplements, but now I was to undergo the agony of physically forcing food into myself. Here is a typical single-day routine:

For breakfast, a grapefruit, a plate of cereal, at least three eggs and bacon followed by toast, marmalade and coffee. Immediately I arrived at the gym to start work at ten o'clock I would have two pints of milk and two cartons of yoghurt. For lunch, between 12.30

and one o'clock I would go to the restaurant on the corner and have
a full three course meal often followed by cheese and biscuits. Half
way through the afternoon there would be more milk and yoghurt.
Mid-evening I would have a full protein dinner consisting of meat,
fish or chicken followed by fruit, ice cream and coffee. Quite often
I would then be forced to have sandwiches before I went to bed.
I suppose I was getting through in a span of something like fifteen
hours enough food to have kept an Indian family of four alive for a
week. The additional vitamins I was taking were vitamins E and C
and the only relief was that I wasn't also being subjected to the B12
injections I had been having earlier.

Of course there was no compulsion. I could have quit at any time
I pleased. But Buster was my coach and as long as I wished the
arrangement to continue I was prepared to accept his training and
diet schedules. Nor did I cheat. When he asked me what I'd had for
breakfast I would tell him exactly. I couldn't lie to him so, instead,
I did exactly what he said. To a compulsive eater I suppose it would
have been one step from heaven but I found the whole process
nauseating, particularly when it came to the milk and yoghurt
routines mid-morning and mid-afternoon. I was already so full that
it was sometimes almost impossible to get them down. To aid my
digestion, which at times felt as though it was going through a
series of 24-hour strikes, Buster arranged for me to have a rest in
the afternoons. There was a large old safe in a nearby car showrooms
and he arranged for me to go there, complete with a lilo and blankets, so that I could lie down in complete seclusion. In theory it
was probably fine but in practice it did nothing for me at all. I
always felt desperately overfull and, despite all the blankets, it was
invariably too cold for me to drop off to sleep. I used to lie there in
the murky darkness imagining that spiders were slowly wending
their way down from the ceiling.

There were two other disadvantages. As any housewife will confirm the food bills shot up astronomically. Buster certainly paid for
the milk and the yoghurt but all the other meals were paid for out
of my own pocket. I came very close, literally, to eating my full
salary every week. And soon came the problem that I no longer had
any clothes at all that would fit me. I needed a completely new
wardrobe. Nor was it the kind of wardrobe that you can buy off the
peg. The combination of huge intakes of food and the murderous

weight-training programme I was undergoing each evening meant that I really was developing the kind of shape that would defeat any multiple tailor. In the upper arms and around the shoulders I was developing so disproportionately to the rest of my body that I was beginning to take on the shape of that Superman chap who kept diving off skyscrapers in all the American comics.

One afternoon, not long before leaving for Jamaica, I went out shopping with Buster's wife to buy the prettiest dress I could possibly find, if only just to make me feel completely feminine again. It was probably the lowest point of my life. I tried on everything I liked. Nothing at all would zip up. If a dress fitted me round the neck and across the shoulders then it hung out over my hips like a bell-tent. If it fitted me round the hips then there was no chance that it would ever reach round my shoulder blades. I bought nothing and went home in despair and cried myself to sleep. I adore lovely clothes.

I suppose I was the only athlete to turn up for the Commonwealth Games in West Indies wearing cast-off maternity clothes. Margaret looked out all the blouses and skirts she had stored away since her last confinement and with a few alterations here and there we somehow got a wardrobe together. At least the blouses fitted me across the back and there was room to tuck them into the skirts.

There remained the problem of a light topcoat. At the very height of my depression I had seen a woman crossing a Belfast street wearing the most elegant white coat and it became almost an obsession to go out and buy one exactly like it. It was hopeless. Eventually I found a white coat of sorts in the cheapest of chain-stores which more or less went round me. I bought it. But in a rage of temper one day I said to Buster, 'I'm now having to go out and get the cheapest rubbish on the market because of what you're doing to me.' Buster was quite unmoved. He had decided on his course of action. My weight, in a matter of months, had soared up from my usual ten stones six pounds to thirteen stone four. It wasn't fat, it was muscle. I hated every minute of the whole detestable operation.

The alternative would have been to have taken steroids, small pills which have the same effect as huge quantities of food. The fact is that at the time, 1966, I knew nothing about steroids at all. Naturally I know a good deal about them now because in recent years they have become a major subject for discussion and their use, rightly, has been universally condemned. It is widely believed that their use, certainly in the vast quantities in which some athletes are supposed to take them, can cause sexual impotence. It was not because of this, however that I resolved not to take them at any point in my career in athletics. Nor, indeed, was it anything as highly principled as the fact that it was blatantly cheating. My mother's death from cancer had left me with a horror of introducing into my body any element of an untested drug which could give me the same disease. I felt that if steroids could achieve rapid muscular growth they could also cause rapid cancer cell growth, which may have no basis in scientific reasoning but was enough to convince me to leave them alone. I appreciate that my argument may seem inconsistent when I was already taking the contraceptive pill during particular stages of the athletic year in order to regulate menstruation during training spells or major competition. The difference was that The Pill had been checked out for side-effects over long periods of research whereas steroids hadn't, and still haven't, been sufficiently investigated in the laboratory to determine exactly what short and long term effects they can have.

There were certainly plenty of rumours about what they could do to the woman athlete and, although they may amount to nothing more than old wives' tales, I had no intention of risking turning into a man.

I am fully aware that a well-known British coach put the story round that I was a steroid-taker. He apparently refused to believe that I could put on almost an additional three stones in muscular weight in a single summer in any other way. Well, athletics can be a bitchy world and perhaps he couldn't think of any other reason why I was continually improving. I am not sure what his motive was but his allegations made me very angry.

As it happens I have no categorical proof of any British woman athlete taking steroids. If they do so they certainly do not advertise the fact. It is well known, of course, that the same cannot be said of all our men athletes. It definitely couldn't be said of American male athletes. Not long ago a medical research team in the United States attempted to set up extensive research into the effects of steroids on weight-lifters and throwers only to discover that there were so few who *weren't* taking them that they couldn't establish any worthwhile comparisons.

To the lay observer, of whom I am one, the calculated decision to juggle with the metabolism of the human body, whether by the employment of anabolic steroids or the massive infusion of food, is probably a repulsive process far removed from any idealism we may have about the values of sport. This, of course, is an idealistic view which is not difficult to preach from the spectators' side of the fence. In the arena it is a different matter altogether. Mary's apparently meek submission to her coach's wishes seem to contradict the strong, independent streak in her nature. What, in fact, she was submitting to was Buster McShane's awareness that by the mid 'sixties many nations were tampering with athletes' bodies to achieve the extra centimetre in the field, or eliminate the split second on the track, which by now could mean the difference between a gold and silver medal, or between the bronze and no medal at all. Quite often the psychological damage so far outweighed any physical advantage that the whole exercise became pointless. This, as we shall see shortly, proved to be the case with Mary Peters at the Jamaica Commonwealth Games. Nevertheless it was a process experienced by almost every major athlete whose career was long enough to stretch from the late 1950's to the early 1970's. While there were doctors and research scientists working flat out on athletic performance programmes both behind the Iron Curtain and in America, Britain could not entirely ignore the trend. By 1966, anyway, no one was even prepared to accept the woman athlete's word for it that she wasn't really a man.

To a girl who had been brought up in the sheltered environment that I had the news that greeted us as soon as we arrived in Kingston, Jamaica, came as a bit of a shock. We had to submit ourselves to sex tests. We giggled about it and made lots of jokes which I shan't repeat here in case this book should fall into the hands of Mrs Mary Whitehouse or be banned from those countries which still regard the human body as something indecent when not almost completely covered by clothes. I forget exactly which room of which building we were instructed to report to, but until we'd been there we couldn't take part in the Games.

By this stage I was something of an old hand on the circuit but that didn't alter factors about my upbringing. Explicit sex education at any school I had ever been to was out of the question. We probably got around to the birds and the bees in biology classes but that would have been the strength of it. I must have been quite eighteen or nineteen before I discovered what homosexuals got up to and I was even older than that when I heard the word lesbian for the first time.

Obviously you cannot be a woman athlete for very long before you discover you have certain problems to contend with which never bother men. Very early in my career I met Dr Wilson Johnson, of Queen's University, Belfast, who is now retired. He was a kind and gentle man and was extremely advanced in his field so it was no problem at all for him to prescribe for us a certain tablet which would permit us to go into a major athletics event without any fear of being inconvenienced by a period. I was so innocent at the time that its other effect, which was to stop babies being born, never occurred to me. I must be one of the very few Pill takers who honestly believed it was discovered to help young ladies succeed in athletics. Subsequently we were to receive the very finest medical attention possible at the West Middlesex Hospital in London where Doctors Andrew and David, whose surnames I must not mention, talked to us in our own language, which was down to earth and so expert that it filled us with confidence. Respectively specialists in gynaecology and muscular troubles, they have done more for British women's athletics than a lot of people whose names are regularly seen in the newspapers. Before any major event every athlete had the most exhaustive medical check-up and if any treatment were required it would be provided on the spot. Marea Hartman was completely responsible for setting up this outstanding service and it has proved to be one of the major developments of recent years.

But I digress. There we were in the corridor outside that forbidding room in Jamaica. All the British teams, Northern Ireland, England, Scotland and Wales and the rest of them, had been summoned together to prove our womanhood in the eyes of the world.

Nowadays these are quite routine matters and no one gives a damn about them but at the time, I must confess, there was a certain amount of embarrassment. We were all there in our housecoats, women of thirty-five and schoolgirls of sixteen, waiting to be examined like the female black slaves of the Deep South more than a hundred years earlier. We were due to go in, one by one, in alphabetical order so I knew I had quite a long wait.

We got away to a bad start. A woman doctor emerged and said in an overbrisk voice, rather like one of those lady doctors from nasty German concentration camps, 'If any of you have got knickers on go and take them off.' Well, for God's sake, we all had knickers on, and bra's too, because this was the middle of the afternoon and streaking had not yet been invented. We all looked at one another somewhat sheepishly and then went back to our rooms and returned, starkers under our housecoats. This is where a woman like Marea Hartman proved her worth. Instead of getting all uptight on our behalf she proceeded to make a huge joke of the whole thing. She produced a cine-camera – to this day I don't know whether it had any film in it – and proceeded to shoot us in extravagant poses. Some played Mata Hari, some Lady Hamilton and a few of the brave ones actually unknotted their housecoats and gave the camera a quick 'flash' in the dirty raincoat tradition. It all helped to break the ice while we sat there like battery hens awaiting our fate.

Eventually the names began to be called and one by one the victims went in. They did not, we noticed, emerge smiling. They flew out of the door and rushed straight back to their quarters. No-one gave us a hint about the kind of procedure we might expect. Some looked distraught, some were clearly upset. What the hell went on in there? We just had to wait our turn and see. The wait was so long that all sorts of things began to play on my mind. So far as I knew, being the possessor of two breasts and one vagina, I was a woman. But what was all this about? What were they investigating? Why was everyone fleeing so hurriedly? Other questions began to fill the mind: what if there is something *different* about me? Am I normal? Is it possible, knowing that many people have suffered as a result of an imperfect hormone balance, that there could be something wrong with me? I have to confess that as I sat there in that bare corridor the very sight of those girls dashing away without telling us what we had to expect made my heart beat a great deal faster.

At last my name was called. I went into a bare room which contained two women doctors, one examination couch and one large enamel bowl containing some white, cloudy antiseptic in which the doctors apparently washed their hands after each examination. What occurred next I can only describe as the most crude and degrading experience I have ever known in my life. I was ordered to lie on the couch and pull my knees up. The doctors then proceeded to undertake an examination which, in modern parlance, amounted to a grope. Presumably they were searching for hidden testes. They found none and I left. Like everyone else who had fled that detestable room I said nothing to anyone still waiting in the corridor and made my way, shaken, back to my room.

That was the first of several sex test examinations and I suppose it was the initial shock which made it so awful. The next one was at the European Championships in Budapest and, while it was scarcely more dignified, at least we knew what to expect. This time we went into an ante-room in pairs removed our clothes, draped them over chairs and proceeded through another door at the far end of the room into an examination hall where no fewer than ten doctors were waiting to give us the once-over. It was so overwhelming that I can't recall whether they were all women, all men or a combination of both. All I do remember is that as we entered we were clutching our passports. I can't remember where I held mine but I do know that, once again, it made you feel as though you were being auditioned for some pretty seamy strip-show. I've never quite discovered what they hoped to establish by all this, apart from seeing every woman competitor parade naked before them, but maybe they were just looking to see if we had hair on our chests. Happily we did not. By now all the reporters had cottoned on to what was happening and they were waiting outside the building to fire off some stories about our most embarrassing moments. To foil them most of the British girls got together and we emerged singing 'We're all queers together' to that lovely tune more commonly associated with the Eton Boating Song.

Down the years the whole procedure was to become somewhat more sophisticated but, at the same time, a little more sinister. By the Mexico Olympics of 1968 they had ostensibly developed a method of determining sex by saliva tests. This was altogether more acceptable from the personal point of view, but before they started I went to Marea Hartman to demand to know what would happen to any of our girls if they *did* fail a test which was now decided by chromosome analysis. It was all very well to say that all this was being done in the name of fair play in sport, but there were serious social implications as well. Supposing a girl just failed the test and was eliminated from the Games in a blaze of world-wide publicity?

She may well have been leading a perfectly balanced life until that moment, with boyfriends and marriage prospects, only to be exposed to millions of people as a freak. Again, supposing the examining doctors made a mistake? A life could be ruined in the very brief time it would take for the news to leak out. As captain of the team my suggestion was that all our girls should be protected by a plan to have them taken to an isolation ward of a hospital should the chromosome tests show up any irregularities. The announcement could then be made that she had contracted some contagious illness and we would then just pray that our word would be accepted. Happily I was worrying unnecessarily as far as the British team were concerned but I think my concern was justified when one of our overseas opponents failed to pass the test. I still believe most strongly that, while sex tests are necessary, they must be conducted with the utmost discretion to avoid causing very great distress.

At least, after Mexico, I had a certificate to prove my womanhood but somehow I came to lose that vital piece of paper before the Munich Olympics. By now the examination process had become still more sophisticated. They now removed a hair from your head to examine the follicle and this, apparently, told them all they wanted to know. Unfortunately it didn't always work with hair that had been bleached or permed and once again a number of girls had to go through agonies of suspense while they were recalled to take a saliva test as well.

It is satisfying to know, of course, that when you've been beaten you've been beaten by a genuine woman. This wasn't always the case in my career before the introduction of sex tests and it may just be significant that two of my opponents in those early days dropped out of international competition altogether when they knew they would have to submit themselves to independent examination. I have no intention of mentioning their names because if my doubts are justified I have nothing but sadness for the effect it must have had on their lives outside sport.

Mary's compassion is probably born of her own experiences in that distressing year of her forced body-building diet, 1966. She had had a season's rest after the 1964 Tokyo Olympics and returned to the athletics scene in 1966 full of vigour and ambition. It proved to be one of the unhappiest and most disappointing of her life.

I cannot recall those Commonwealth Games in Jamaica with any affection at all. I had limited myself to a single event, the shot, and set my sights on a single target, the gold medal. After all that agonising preparation I should have won it, but I didn't. My main rival there was Val Young, the New Zealander, and at a pre-Games meeting I beat her easily. I shot-put 56 ft, which was fully three feet more than Val, and it really should have given me the kind of psychological advantage to make me invincible. Even now I cannot fully analyse what went wrong on the big day except to know that I was irritable and distracted and quite unable to get myself into a winning mood. The very last straw came when the day's programme went haywire and the shot competition started an hour later than scheduled. I desperately wanted to get on with it but I had to wander around instead. It was during that hour's wait that I lost the gold. My concentration went and the adrenalin seemed to dry up and when the time came I was quite incapable of pulling out the big one. I had to be content with the silver.

I was furious with myself at being so mentally weak. But my own annoyance was nothing compared with Buster's wrath. Far from sparing me any sympathy he stormed out of the stadium without saying a single word to me. In his view I had let myself, him and Northern Ireland down and wasted a complete summer's work.

I rang him at his hotel and he refused to come to the phone to talk. I left a message that I would like him there when I went up to receive my silver medal. He refused to come to that ceremony either. I then went to his hotel and once more he refused to see me. Eventually, of course, he couldn't avoid me any longer. I made the mistake of putting on an almost light-hearted pose. 'Ah, well,' I said, 'I expect there are a few people somewhere who still love me.' That made him even more livid and I walked into a force-ten dressing down. 'That's your trouble,' he said, 'you can take defeat too lightly.' It was the start of a long lecture about mental attitudes. The difference between us was that I was very disappointed but wanted to conceal it. Buster was very disappointed and didn't care who knew. Eventually I said to him, 'If you react like this again I shall finish with athletics altogether.' Unlike the occasion when he struck me in training, it did not provoke an apology. He said nothing, only glowered. He came to realise, in the end, that I was as upset as he was.

As usual, Buster was right. I had talent, I had strength and I trained religiously. But until I hardened my mental approach I was always going to be the bridesmaid, the runner-up, the silver medallist, the second best.

It was too late to work on a fundamental change of character in that season of 1966. There were still the European Championships to come and I almost felt doomed before I competed. My failure in Jamaica had a paralysing effect on me. At my best I should have given the formidable Miss Chizhova a very good fight but my defences were down. She won the shot with 56 ft 6 in and I trailed in almost eight feet behind her. The year was a write-off and I was beginning to wonder whether there were enough years left.

7. Mexico: Myth and Reality

The pentathlon, by definition, is five times as strenuous as most events in women's athletics. Mary found it essential to work only in alternate years in competition. She did little on the track in 1965, following the Tokyo Olympics. She again did little in 1967, following her disastrous Commonwealth Games in Jamaica. The year 1968 was probably the watershed of her life in sport. She began preparing for it on November 21, 1967, which was as grey as any other day in that early Belfast winter. All over the world her rivals for the Mexico Olympics were doing the same. Unlike some of them, in the American colleges and the Iron Curtain state squads, Mary had to hold down a job while going into training. What that training comprised may surprise those armchair experts who turn a switch and criticise the efforts of British athletes on television. At random from Mary's papers I have chosen just one document which she received from Buster McShane. It is merely an extract from the training programmes he had devised for her. To most people it will be gibberish. It may just be fascinating gibberish to anyone who seriously would like to know how an Olympic champion is made. This, abbreviated, was one week's programme:

FRIDAY: *Usual warm-up plus relax sprint arm movement and ankle rotations. Sprint starts giving five feet. Long jump: four from four strides off board for maximum height, three from six strides off board, two from eight feet holding height intro to extend landing. Relaxed full run-up, jumping emphasis on technique not distance. Two or three relaxed running with just one 20 yard period around 80 yards out with 90 per cent acceleration holding relaxed slightly wider arm action.*

SATURDAY: *High jump with warm-up leading into crabs bend and hypering on to landing area plus vertical jumps to mark on handball net. Four four-stride jumps over 4 ft 10 in. 5 ft 2 in for three clean jumps concentrating on steady stride pattern with 6–7–8 count at take-*

off. Emphasis on fast 7 to counter fault of long stride hindering quadriceps drive with late and low pelvis position. Be conscious of (a) a fair pause between jumps, control adrenalin flow and hold relaxation and (b) you will always tend to be close in at take-off and must observe this and related good continual arc. Increase bar by one inch and jump as in competition until 5 ft 6 in and really concentrate for three good clearances. This is more important than stabs at greater heights. On specific days I'll set it to 5 ft 8 in with a side bet (smile). Hurdle work as it has now developed. We want a sharper, more forward action of your lead arm and head following it. Lack of this is partly caused by too much tension in your mastoids and trapezius is hindering your lead leg to drive smoothly but quicker to the ground. Thus just a little more flexibility in the trailing leg's adductors allowing a more rapid whip-up of the knee will get you into the 13.4's now that the new eight stride approach is eventually settling in. Shot repetition, free glides relaxed but lower than normal followed by four stands and two glides. Then six puts all measured. These you can follow some days with three stands, really coming out after it, and three similar six inch shortened glides.

SUNDAY: *Build up as you feel best for long-jump, utilising, of course, 10 stride marker and develop a count-in. Keep the shoulders relaxed. Allow yourself six full run-up jumps, but remember your preparations must see your best jump in the first three. After that I would like to see you do glides with 12 lb shot aiming for 45 ft, finishing with six stands with 16. We then start striding and two starts, followed by two 50-yards from blocks, two 80's, one easy 120, followed by a time trial 150 and, with full recovery, three-quarters speed through 200 metres.*

WEDNESDAY: *High jump warm-up as before, only four jumps over 5 ft 3 in concentrating on fast quadricep thrust and hyper and leg-flick with far-out take-off. Work on hurdles and starts, ending with three starts over two hurdles and then two and three over three. Finish off with long-jump but don't fatigue on it. Work for just speed and height off board. Don't worry about distance but check last stride length. If you want to do shot keep it to three stands and six glides.*

Buster adds: 'Remind me to review nutrition.'

The discriminating reader will require to know what the hell Mary Peters was wasting her time at on Mondays, Tuesdays and Thursdays. The answer is that she was weight-training according to schedules so complicated that they make the foregoing read like light relief. There is

more to being an athlete than ever comes out of the commentator's
microphone.

By 1968 I was altogether a harder woman, but that was not enough.
I did not win a medal at the Mexico Olympics. By now my greatest
personal rival had departed the scene but new opponents had
emerged. The departure of Mary Rand, stricken by the injury that
hits so many great athletes, saddened me more than I can describe.
I have to examine my soul very carefully before putting that on
record because I knew that, even under new training schedules and
with my new attitude, I would always be hard pressed to beat her in
any competition. With Mary gone, with her dominating personality
lifted from me, I felt that nothing was beyond me but for all that I
took no pleasure in her retirement from athletics.

For reasons I shall mention later Mary had gone to live in
America. She still wanted to represent Britain in the Olympics so she
had to return to qualify. We met at Crystal Palace where I had taken
a week off to train. Poor Mary was very miserable. It was a difficult
period for her domestically, but she was also severely hampered by
Achilles tendon trouble which forced her to go every day for treatment. Already Ann Wilson and I had qualified for the British team
so there was just one place left and it was being kept open until
Mary had competed in an international invitation meeting at which
the selectors could judge her form. On the day Mary could not
compete at all. Sue Scott, meanwhile, competed for England with
real distinction. Still the selectors refused to name the third choice.
This was perhaps hard on Sue, but La Rand was not a lady you just
passed over because of an injury that might heal itself in days or
weeks. Unfortunately this was not the case. They arranged a special
fitness test for her and Mary broke down before it had hardly
started. She tried to hurdle and couldn't. Mary Rand's glittering
athletic career was over. The great challenge to me from within was
over and if there was anyone who felt more awful about it than her
in Great Britain it was me. I would have loved to have beaten her
but I never did and an opponent's withdrawal is no triumph at all.
I can honestly say that being under her shadow for almost seven
years left no scars on me at all.

They made me captain of the British women's team for the
Mexico Olympics. In retrospect I am sorry because it didn't help

my athletics. Then, as now, I have no idea what an athletics captain's responsibilities are supposed to be. Once, captaining a British team in an international match, I actually went to discover what I was supposed to do and the answer was 'Whatever you choose to do.' I appreciated that it was an honour and that it was meant to boost my ego but, frankly, it was nothing more than a damned nuisance. I made sure the girls had their sex tests and turned up at team meetings and received their mail and messages but, in fact, I did nothing that the average hotel porter couldn't do with far more efficiency. A team captain has no authority in matters of conduct or the exercising of discipline. Those are the duties of the team manager. Of course you can urge your compatriots to do their utmost, but they are going to do that anyway so I would suggest the position is somewhat supernumerary. I'm quite relieved to see that more recently no team captains have been appointed.

In this respect athletics is quite different to other sports where captains either dictate tactics during the battle or standards of social behaviour after it. Clearly a pentathlon performer cannot tell an 800 metre runner how to approach a race nor, in my case, would I care to assume the position where I had to tell a responsible colleague how to conduct her life after hours. There is certainly one British newspaper which would have you believe that every Olympic/ Commonwealth/European Games is nothing more than a quadrennial vice-racket promoted for no other reason than to allow between 5000 and 15 000 athletes and officials to engage in adultery and gang-bangs not to mention such refinements as seduction and rape. The author of these ravings happens to be one of the most gentle and kindly men you have ever met. His hobby is growing roses. Of course there is a grain of truth in what he writes. There is as much sexual activity at a major Games as there is at any other congregation of such a large number of men and women. The only problem is that at an event like the Olympics it is much more difficult for a man and lady to get together in some kind of privacy than it is, say, at an annual congress of the National Union of Journalists where the delegates are on expense accounts which permit them unlimited use of their own private rooms. The chances of a male athlete getting into a female athlete's room in a Games Village are absolutely nil. We are guarded, whether we like it or not, more closely than the inmates of a nineteenth century Persian harem.

In the men's quarters, meanwhile, the competitors are mostly quartered four to a room. This, admittedly, does not rule out the possibility of Mr A getting together with Miss B for reasons which could terminate in unbridled passion but it does, you'll probably agree, make it bloody difficult. Messrs B, C and D do tend to object.

If the rose-growing sex investigator feels that I'm trying to deprive him of his living then I freely admit to knowing all about the old elastic-band-on-the-doorhandle trick. This is placed there to warn room mates that it would be indiscreet to enter until the elastic band has been removed. Of course it goes on. What the hell does he expect? But I have never yet been to a Games whch warranted such headlines as 'Sin City' or 'Village of Vice'.

You will, inevitably, come across the big-game hunter bragging of his conquests. I know of one room at one Games where the occupants kept a wall-chart detailing the ladies who had allegedly submitted to their limited charms. I wasn't outraged at all. I just found it rather sad that there were still some men about who found it ego-boosting to embarrass a woman by listing her name in their pathetic scorebooks. In the 1870's it may well have impressed their colleagues. In the 1970's it implies immaturity. If a person has a happy relationship, and I don't pretend that quite a few haven't at international Games, they just don't talk about it.

The cruellest remark I have ever heard at any sports event came from a man who said to a girl: 'That was a lousy excuse you gave for not coming to bed with me last night. You didn't even swim very well.' He happened to be one of the wall-chart men and if he reads this he will know what I mean when I say I hope his luck's changed.

I also hope that any parents reading this won't leap to the conclusion that young lady athletes are in moral danger the moment they are chosen to tour abroad. Far from it. Although they are probably unaware of it they are watched over carefully and wisely from the moment they report until the moment they are delivered back to London Airport. The person responsible for this is a quite remarkable woman, the same Marea Hartman who had persuaded me to join Spartan Ladies' Athletic Club. Marea, herself a county sprinter in the era when shorts came down to the knee, became team manager for the Women's AAA in 1950 and full England and British team manager in 1954. Since then I doubt whether there has been a single day in her life in which she hasn't done something for the cause of athletics. She is probably the most indefatigable person, man or woman, I have ever met. You can telephone her at midnight and she's working. You can telephone her again at six a.m. and she's often back at her desk. She loves a drink and she can swear as eloquently as a drill sergeant, as I discovered one day on tour when she slipped in the shower, damaged her back and put her tongue to words which I had literally never heard before. But for sheer commonsense in the handling and protection and encouragement of young athletes she probably has no rival in the world. She thinks young, acts young and accepts every succeeding generation of young athletes as though they are the most important charges ever to come into her keeping. I recall, on one of my earliest trips with her, slipping secretly into her room and pinning up her clothes with safety pins and giving her an apple-pie bed. It seemed pretty hilarious at the time and I suppose Marea has had to put up with that kind of juvenile humour from a long succession of her girls over more than twenty years. But never once have I seen her show any annoyance.

I have many instances of how she won loyalty and established her authority. One night, when we had finished our competition in Belgrade, several of us wanted to go out on what was an unashamed pub crawl with a few of the BBC men. Marea's method was not to forbid us but to come with us. We returned at five o'clock the following morning and flopped into bed. Not Marea. To avoid having to make any complicated explanations to the official with whom she was sharing a room she slipped in quietly, had a shower and went straight to work. It was always assumed that she and her girls had had a good night's sleep.

She had an anxious moment during the Tokyo Olympics when Linda Knowles, the youngest member of the team, still hadn't reported back at ten o'clock at night. Two of us pulled on our track suits, borrowed bikes and went out to search for her. We found her chatting quite innocently to some members of the Swedish team and brought her back to our quarters. This incident received quite a deal of publicity in the British Press but Marea's method of dealing with it was interesting. The following evening we were being entertained long and lavishly by the British Embassy. At ten o'clock precisely a car arrived to collect Linda Knowles. 'Quite late enough for you, dear,' said Marea, making her point. The incident was

closed and the big stick had never been wielded. When we got back
to London Airport Linda's parents were there to thank Marea for
what she had done.

I have good reason to know a great deal about Marea's many
personal kindnesses and so have many others. She repeatedly flew
out to Dr Issels's clinic to see Lillian Board during the last months
of Lillian's terrible illness. She never allows a week to pass without
calling in with a bottle of sherry and an evening meal for Teddy
Knowles, the founder of the Spartan club, who is now eighty-five.
She alone set up the superb free medical scheme now available to
every British international woman athlete. And if it ever happens
that one of her girls looks like being done down by officialdom or
rivals in some overseas meeting she becomes a complete tigress.

Over the years, during which we have become very close personal
friends, only one thing has amazed me about Marea: her complete
incomprehension of even the simplest mechanical device. Loading
a camera or using a record player is utterly beyond her. She must
also be the only woman in Europe who possesses an ultra modern
automatic washing machine which she has never used. 'I haven't
the faintest idea how it works,' she says. 'I just bung my stuff in a
bag, take it round to the launderette and eat fish and chips while
it's being done.' On the other hand there are few women who have
vaulted over a ten foot wall to get out of a stadium when everyone has
gone and the place has been locked up. That's what she did on my
first overseas trip with her and it was the start of a lifetime friendship
which I treasure greatly.

But I have been diverted along the road to the Mexico Olympics.
Much controversy surrounded these Games, from the altitude at
which they were staged, via the brutal crushing of a student demonstration to the Black Power demonstrations for which they became
memorable to some and infamous to others. Curiously we knew less
about the shootings than people back in Britain. We were not
allowed to leave the Village unescorted and we weren't getting
newspapers from home. The trip began inauspiciously for me
when I glanced out of the aircraft window about an hour out of
London and noticed some rather disturbing black smoke pouring
out of one of the engines. We turned around, landed quite safely at
Heathrow and then set out again some three hours later. For me
things never really recovered from that false start. I strained an

ankle some days before the start of the pentathlon, told no one in case it should be interpreted as an excuse and finished a disappointing ninth. Unless I look up the records now I remember very little of how I fared in each event. For all the hard work I had done these were never going to be my Games. Ingrid Becker won the event and since she finished 295 points ahead of me I could only offer genuine congratulations to a long-time opponent. For me it was back to the drawing board.

I was fortunate then and, indeed, through most of my career, in that no one really expected me to win. To go to an Olympic Games as a white-hot hope is an agonising experience and I do wish, though probably vainly, that sportswriters would realise this before they brand anyone as 'favourite' to win a medal. Men like David Bedford and the American, Jim Ryun, could write volumes on this subject. This kind of treatment can pressurise a sensitive person almost out of their minds. One person who suffered badly in Mexico was the late Lillian Board who had been made 'favourite' to win a 400 metres gold medal weeks before she left her home in Ealing. The pressures on her became so great that throughout the whole of those Games we very rarely saw her in the Olympic Village except at bedtimes. She went out with her father and close friends early most mornings and returned late at night simply to escape the constant hounding and interviews. In the end she won the silver medal but I shall always be convinced that the gold would have been hers had she not been the victim of a huge press build-up before her event.

An even more frightening example of this in Mexico concerned the Jugoslavian 800 metres runner, Vera Nikolic, whose compatriots were so positive that she would win the gold they actually prepared a special issue of a postage stamp which was to be put on sale throughout the country the day after her triumph. Perhaps only another athlete can understand the fearful pressures that subjected her to. In the event she did not even reach the final. She ran off the track during her semi-final and was so mentally disturbed at the thought of the reaction back home that later that day she attempted to kill herself by throwing herself from a bridge. Fortunately she was seen and saved. I would like to think the lesson of that near tragedy has been learned by the media, but unfortunately it hasn't.

8. The Road to Munich

Most leading athletes, like all top cricketers, can reel off the outstanding statistics of their careers as easily as the rest of us can recite the opening couplets of the traditional nursery rhymes. The engaging Derek Ibbotson, for example, can probably tell you the first 50 four-minute miles, in exact sequence, without pausing for breath. Freddie Trueman would certainly be able to tell you his precise bowling figures in any Test match in which he ever played. It is a revealing aspect of Mary Peters' personality that she is virtually incapable of recalling any of her own times and distances without recourse to the record books. She has an almost infallible memory for people's names, the colour of their hair, the ages of their children, their telephone numbers and their amusing idiosyncrasies. In the early spring of 1970, following a year's rest after the Mexico Olympics, she equalled the world indoor 60 metres hurdles record at Cosford. After the disappointments of the Commonwealth Games in Jamaica and the Mexico Olympics she was desperately looking for some such encouragement to help her through the endless training necessary to prepare for the next two big events, the Edinburgh Commonwealth Games of 1970 and the Munich Olympics of 1972. I asked her for the record time she had achieved. She thought with visible concentration. 'I don't remember,' she finally said. Then she added: 'Really, those things have never mattered very much to me. I've just enjoyed meeting all the people.'

The Cosford record, whatever it was, really did give me a boost when I badly needed one. Four years earlier I had begun to feel that time was running out and here was another Olympics gone with nothing more than pleasure and self-satisfaction to show for it. One year to the day, exactly, before the Edinburgh Games I got down to training again and this time I was determined that it would be gold or bust. Anyway, I knew I had a chance. Mary Rand had departed and for the first time my own specialist event, the pentathlon, was to be included in a Commonwealth meeting. True, they had made a few amendments to it. The hurdles now were to be 100 metres instead of 80 and both Buster and I thought this would be to my disadvantage as it would mean a complete revision of my stride pattern. I'm notorious for my short strides and I thought this would mean a great problem fitting in the paces between the hurdles, but it was surprisingly simple. I had to change my starting leg and amend the run to the first hurdle but I became accustomed to that very swiftly and was soon very confident. The year's rest and the Cosford record and the easy way in which I had adapted to the new hurdles all did a great deal for my confidence which had taken such a battering. In fact, even then, my horizon lifted from the immediate challenge of Edinburgh to the one beyond, Munich.

I had less success trying to change my high-jumping style to the straddle method, mainly because we still didn't have ideal conditions to work in in Northern Ireland. Instead of the soft-landing pits I was falling into sand and jarring every bone in my body. So I abandoned that, went back to the old half Western Roll, half Mary Peters style of jumping and didn't look back. Another record came my way when I set up a new points total for a British pentathlon and was rewarded by one of our officials snidely asking me: 'What were the officials like?' Since this was tantamount to implying that somebody had been cheating I whispered, 'I'll bloody show you, mate,' and I did.

In winning the gold at Edinburgh I set up a new record for both the United Kingdom and the Commonwealth with 5148 points. I was delighted about that and I was naturally very happy to win the first gold of what was now becoming a long career. Yet, for all that, I was overtaken by the same feeling that comes back to me now as I try to recall my emotions in the Meadowbank Stadium that day. Any euphoria was very much kept in check by the thought that this was still a long way from an Olympic medal. I certainly have no intentions of disparaging achievements in the Commonwealth Games but, really, my own achievements had been quite unspectacular. I had to put up with a certain amount of gamesmanship and, being a member of the Northern Ireland team, I had other events on my mind as well. In fact in the space of three days I took part in all five pentathlon events, the heats and finals of the hurdles and the qualifying round and finals of the shot, which is somewhat strenuous. Yet the prevailing memories now are less of wild jubilation over the fact that I had won at last than of stirring the crowd up to perform the slow handclap when the officials were dreadfully slow in getting the 200 metres underway and of complaining bitterly when told that I would have to hang around the stadium because Prince Charles was going to present my medal and he hadn't arrived yet. I was about to claim that I don't know what was wrong with me that day, but I do know precisely. I was now impatient for real success and Munich, still two years away, had become an obsession.

One of the happy outcomes of Edinburgh was that Mike Bull, a tall and sensitive young Belfast philosophy student, joined me under the coaching of Buster McShane. Mike had won the pole vault gold for Northern Ireland and Buster had great ambitions to turn him into a decathlete as well. It was strange that such an outstanding coach and such an outstanding athlete had taken so long to come together in a provincial city, but I suspect Mike, like so many people, was very wary of Buster's methods and possibly his motives as well. Any reservations Mike had were soon gone. He was astounded at Buster's enormous knowledge. Mike's arrival was a fortunate day for me. Training can become a lonely, weary business and training together we revived one another's interest and enthusiasm. He was particularly good to me during the tragedy that, within three years, was to overtake us both.

But for the moment we were working with a single objective in mind: the 1972 Olympics. What I needed, I knew, was a chance I had never yet had of being about to get down to solid, full-time training, uninterrupted by work or any other distractions. Many of my Munich opponents, I knew, would take full-time training for granted and all I wanted, even if only for a short period, was an equal opportunity. My main activity in 1971 was to set out to see how it could be achieved. This brought me to the door of 10 Queen Street, Mayfair, the offices of the Winston Churchill Memorial Trust.

Already Buster had applied for a Churchill Scholarship to go to the United States and write a book about social behaviour. When he didn't get one, or even the interview that might lead to one, he reacted quite predictably in announcing that it was quite obvious that the Trust had a personal vendetta against him and that they could go and get stuffed. Buster always reacted like that when he lost. It made him all the keener that I should apply for one though, in the very next breath, he was saying it was perfectly obvious that if he hadn't succeeded then I had no chance at all. I knew, though, that a great number of British athletes and coaches, including Mike Bull, had been financed through America by the Churchill Trust so I applied for an interview and got it.

I've never greatly enjoyed interviews of this kind and this one was no exception. The interviewers included the inevitable man in a pair of Alec Douglas-Home spectacles, Lord Byers whom I recognised too late and Colin Cowdrey, the cricketer, whom I recognised instantly. They seemed in some doubt for a while about which of the scholarship courses I was applying for. Was it Docks and Docking? Was it Sculpture? Was it Nursery School Teaching? 'No,' I said, 'it is Participation in Sport.' They didn't look very impressed. What objective did I have in mind? 'Well,' I said, 'I think I can win a gold medal in the Munich Olympics. If I could just get away from the tensions of Belfast for a while and settle down to regular hard training somewhere where the weather is good, I honestly think I've got a chance.' They weren't very impressed with that either. Wasn't I a bit long in the tooth to harbour ambitions like that? Hadn't I been in athletics rather too long? Didn't I think I was setting my sights just a little too high? 'No, no, no,' I replied, but I could see from their faces that they weren't very convinced. I was applying for an £800 grant, far less than had been handed out to other sportsmen and coaches in the past, and the discussion about it went on so long that there was one point where I was on the verge of telling them to forget the whole thing and apologise for troubling them. Eventually, and very sceptically, they agreed that I should go.

'How did you get on?' asked Buster. 'Dead easy,' I said, 'they begged me to take the money.'

I went to Pasadena, in California, to stay with good friends, Bill and Judy Pearl. Bill's name will be well known to anyone who has followed body-building for he was twice a Mr Universe, once when he was quite young and again when he was forty-one years of age, which was a remarkable achievement in a highly competitive business. He is an extremely modest man who is totally dedicated not only to his own sport but to promoting good health among other people. He ran his own gymnasium and was up every morning at four a.m. to train there for three and a half hours before coming back to take Judy and me for breakfast and then getting down to his own day's work. This, among many other things, included running a fitness course for the locally stationed officials of the American Space Programme.

It was heaven. It was also three and a half months before the start of the Olympics and exactly the perfect time to go into full work. I had never known anything like it before. All I had to do was eat and sleep and train. The sun shone every day, the excellent track of the Pasadena City College was within walking distance down the road, there was Bill's gymnasium to work-out in and once a week a friend, John Forde, used to drive me to train on the UCLA tartan track in Los Angeles. Everyone was kind and I phoned Buster with ecstatic reports about the progress I was making. I was so on top of the world that in Los Angeles I indulged in some real showing-off. I asked a girl athlete if she minded whether I trained with her and she said, 'You're Mary Peters, aren't you? I used to do the pentathlon myself.' I thought I would show her what a real pentathlete looked like. I stood quite still and put the shot 47 ft. If it startled me it startled that poor girl still more. I then proceeded to put it properly around 55 ft, trying to look as though I did that sort of thing in training every day of the week. There had to be some retribution for that kind of meanness on my part and when it came it knocked me sideways.

Overnight I developed the dreaded Achilles tendon trouble. It began as a nagging pain and gradually got worse and worse until, in the end, I was at screaming pitch. I couldn't bear to touch either ankle with even a finger. I had over trained.

I didn't know how to begin to tell Buster what had happened. In a couple of my phone calls back to Belfast I pretended that all was still going well but it was pointless trying to keep up the pretence. I phoned him one evening and sobbed my heart out. 'I can't stay any longer,' I said, 'my ankles are so sore that I simply can't run any longer.' I have never been more distressed in my sports career. For the first occasion in my life I had the time yet I couldn't do anything with it. Buster's reaction was typical. 'I shall be out on the next plane,' he said. In just under twenty-four hours he was in Pasadena.

Buster walked into the apartment and barely spared the time to go through the courtesies of saying hello to anyone. 'Get me your training shoes,' he said. I laid them all out on the table. 'Which ones have you been using most?' he demanded. I pointed to the pair I had used almost constantly. They fitted snugly round the back of the foot and had built-up heels. I had chosen them deliberately because I thought this design would take some of the strain off my legs. Buster examined them closely and then took them across the room and hurled them in the waste-bin. 'Now,' he said, 'we'll go and do some running.' He took me down to the track and made me run, gently, on the grass. It was excruciating agony, just like jabbing something into the exposed nerve of a tooth. I cried with the pain of it all the time and I cried the next day and the next and the day after that when Buster took me back, making me go through it again and again, building up the distance all the time.

Bill Pearl and his wife watched it all in silent amazement. They clearly saw Buster as a complete monster. They said nothing. And by the end of a week Buster was proved right. The fluid was moving away from the back of the foot and slowly the pain began to ease. It still hurt but I could live with it. There was one other small problem to overcome. To reduce the inflammation in the leg a doctor had prescribed some tablets without warning me that it would build up fluid in the body. In the space of ten days I put on one and a half stones and became so bloated that if you pressed your finger against my body it would leave a deep indentation. I could only think that I must have been overeating, because of my anxiety. Buster stopped that, too. I went on to a course of diuretics and in a few days was back to normal.

Physically I had lost valuable time in my preparation but mentally I am not so sure that that distressing period did not actually do good. I was flooded with relief to know that I wasn't, after all, going to miss the Games and I was filled with a determination the like of which I had never known before. Buster and I flew home to Belfast together and within a couple of days I did a pentathlon, all in one evening, on the worn-out track at Queen's University. I achieved a good score and I knew that the Churchill Scholarship had paid off. Two years later, as a former Churchill Scholar, I was invited to present Lady Churchill with a bouquet on her birthday.

Two other things happened before the Olympics. Buster, as I

have written before, knocked me down. And competing in the long jump at Crystal Palace, where I was keen to win a prize of a Philips cassette tape-recorder, I injured my ankle. It was exactly seven days before we were due to leave. Not until long afterwards did I realise how serious it was. I was saved by Dr David (whose surname his profession forbids me to reveal) who injected so accurately into the ligament that I barely thought about it again.

Thus it was, after some alarums and excursions, that I went into battle at the Munich Olympics.

9. *Survival of the Fittest*

The long Veronica Lake hairstyle, the soft, gentle voice, the concern for humanity, the self-deprecating humour conceal in Mary Peters what sportswriters, for want of precise psychological definition, call 'the killer streak.' It is there, all right.

The really big occasion doesn't exactly bring out the most noble traits of the human character. I recognised that in myself and I certainly saw it in other people even before we got into the stadium for the opening day's events in the pentathlon. The official car due to take us across the zig-zagging mile from the Village didn't show up so we tried hitching a lift in the cars of other pentathletes, all of whom were sitting there looking about as tense as I was. Not one of them would stop. I asked an Australian team manager if we could share a ride in their minibus which had enough room for a small army. The answer was an adamant 'No.' Charity really began at home that morning. So we had to go through the infernal torture of catching one camp bus down to the security gates and then changing into another which stopped and started all the way across the vast Munich complex with us swaying inside like rush-hour commuters. It was no worse than about five million Londoners go through every morning, I suppose, but on a day when you are looking everywhere for good luck omens it makes you begin to wonder whether Caesar is already beginning to turn his thumbs down.

It wasn't the first irritation. The other one was bigger. The previous evening, when the draw for the heats of the 100 metres hurdles was announced, I was staggered to hear I had been placed in the second heat with the slower runners while my own colleague, Ann Wilson, was up there with the very fast runners in the first heat. Only a couple of weeks previously I had run a wind-assisted 13.1 in Edinburgh, which was faster than Ann, and here I was being done down. It wasn't just a matter of pride. It is vital to do well in the opening event of a pentathlon and it is essential to be there with the fastest opponents. The pace is hotter and they 'pull you through' to a better time.

Ann and I were not only team mates but friends, but that did not alter the fact that both Buster and I felt we had been tricked. I was very upset.

I had had to get out of the Village and its claustrophobic atmosphere so Buster and I went into Munich for a quiet meal. Even this proved a disaster when the waiter rendered my kebabs uneatable by pouring pure curry powder over the lot. At least the table proved useful for writing a fairly strongly worded letter of protest about the draw to Arthur Gold, the British manager. We demanded an inquiry and got it. The draw, in fact, had been made by computer but my Edinburgh time of 13·1 hadn't been fed into it. At least this convinced us that there hadn't been any dirty work at the crossroads, but I still felt it was unfair. When Arthur Gold asked me if he could tear up my written protest I said he couldn't. I, too, was in the mood for a little charity starting at home.

It all increased the strain and tension as we set out for the track at the unearthly hour of 7.45 a.m. The hurdles were due at 9.30, a ridiculous time to expect one's concentration to be totally set. It was hard to fight off the feeling that nothing was working out. The only consolation I could find was in the number pinned to my back – 111 – and the fact that it had been handed to me by a man named Gold. Three firsts and a gold medal would suit me well, I thought. Around me in the indoor warm-up area there were twenty-nine other women pentathletes assembled from all over the world who would settle for that as well.

The sight, as we came down through the competitors' tunnel into the arena, was staggering. Already there were 25 000 spectators in their seats. Within an hour it was jammed to the eaves with 80 000 and by then my black mood had gone. All our fears about the importance of getting into the first heat, though theoretically justified at the time, had proved groundless. Heide Rosendahl, as expected, had won it in 13·34 seconds but my time, in the second heat, was faster. Christine Bodner, the East German, set a terrific pace and I

The Edinburgh Commonwealth Games in 1970. I had to be first in the 200 metres to win the pentathlon gold medal and I just beat Ann Wilson in a new Commonwealth record.

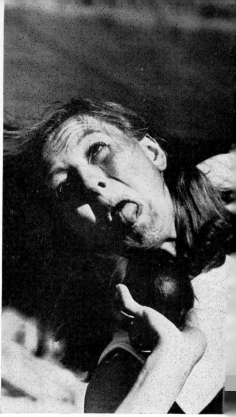

The development of my shot-putting technique. I hated this event and at first tried to perform with as much feminine grace as I could muster, but to be successful I had to introduce determination and effort to a considerable degree so that, as you can see on the facing page, I had to build up the aggression.

Top: At the Munich Olympics getting over the high jump at
1.71 metres. I had knocked the bar off twice and this was my
last attempt at that height. I will never forget the way the crowd
helped my performance in that event.

Bottom: The final of the 200 metres where I had to stay in
touch with Burglinde Pollak. The pain was terrible and I would
never have made it if I had not remembered Buster telling me
that if I pumped with my arms my legs would follow.

kept coming through and coming through on her heels to cross the line in 13·29. It was a fifth of a second better than I had ever run before without wind assistance. Christine's time of 13·25 and mine were both corrected to 13·3 which meant that we had both equalled the Olympic record. It was a jubilant start in the event in which most of the experts had expected me to yield a little ground. So after the hurdles Bodner led with 966 points, I was just six points behind on 960 and the two girls I had always seen as my biggest rivals, Rosendahl and the world-record holder, Burglinde Pollak, were lying third and fourth behind me. Rosendahl had 953 points, Pollak 927 and Ann Wilson was fifth with 916.

It filled me with enormous confidence and determination and that was just as well because enough niggling incidents were happening out there to crack the concentration of a chess master. I do not tell them from any sense of outrage but for the enlightenment of the reader.

One personal crisis was already over for, even before the hurdles, I had fallen foul of the German officials over the matter of my running shoes. Understandably you have to submit your kit for inspection as soon as you get into the track area. They rummage through your bag, searching for things like two-way radios with which you might be contemplating having an illegal chat with your coach. I was able to satisfy them that I was perfectly 'clean' on that count but as soon as I handed over my shoes for examination they shook their heads and told me flatly that I would not be permitted to wear them. They were a new type of shoe, manufactured just before the Games, which had a dozen short plastic wedges in the sole instead of the six conventional spikes. Not only had the manufacturers assured me they were perfectly legal but I knew full well that many athletes had already used them in competition in these very Games. Yet here were mine being rejected. It could have wrecked all my efforts before the first gun went because the chances of being able to borrow another pair which fitted my hardly dainty feet at short notice were remote. Astonishingly I had brought a second pair, fitted with the normal spikes with me. I say astonishingly because it was the first time in all my career that I had taken a reserve pair of shoes to a starting line. To this day I don't know what persuaded me to do it because I had no reason whatever to believe that the first pair would be unacceptable. Perhaps it was the sheer relief that helped me hurdle so well.

At that point it had never occurred to me that certain German officials were doing everything in their power to help their own favourite, Rosendahl, win. But there was soon clear evidence that that was precisely what they were up to.

As soon as the hurdles were over we were herded out of one exit and back up through a series of tunnels under the stands to the point where we were due to be led out into the arena again for the shot. This was the event in which I had to score heavily and knew I could. I had been going well in recent training, with distances of 56 and even 57 ft, and I wanted to get at it quickly before the feeling of well-being inspired by the hurdles wore off. It was important, at least, that I was out there warming-up but again German officialdom intervened. We were kept hanging about in a bunch near the entrance, unable either to communicate with our coaches outside or to get out into the stadium to practise. Suddenly I became suspicious. I started counting. There should have been twenty-nine of us but there were only twenty-seven. And, sure enough, the two missing girls were the West Germans Rosendahl, and her colleague, Karen Mack.

I went up to a German official and demanded: 'Where is Rosendahl?' He shrugged.

In an even less ladylike voice I demanded again: 'Where – is – Rosendahl?' He shrugged again and still said nothing.

It was becoming a rather boring and one-sided conversation, but there were no prizes for politeness at this stage so I almost screamed the question at him a third time. It was what might be described as a rhetorical query. I knew damned well where she was. She and Karen Mack had been quietly slipped away to the neighbouring indoor warm-up area and were working away while the rest of us were stiffening up mentally as well as physically. The Germans were beginning to look rather worried by now as they were fully entitled to. Although I was helpless to do anything about it their little plot was rumbled by Buster, Marea Hartman and John Le Masurier who had gone to the indoor area to meet us. Immediately they saw that only the two West Germans were there, they guessed what was happening. Marea lodged a complaint and the Frauleins Rosendahl and Mack were sent back to join the rest of us.

The difference between shot-putting as an individual competition and shot-putting as one fifth of an Olympic pentathlon is the absolute necessity to eliminate error. You only have three attempts, and if your first put is a foul you have subjected yourself to extreme psychological pressure. The ideal technique is to get a safe one in first and then belt the other two for all you are worth. If you are still going for the safe one with your second throw, you have conceded a big advantage.

Despite all the Goldfinger ploys behind the scenes I still had time for a thorough warm-up out in the stadium. It seemed as though half a lifetime had passed since the start of the hurdles but, in fact, it was less than an hour. I felt confident and I certainly felt aggressive and with the crowd now at its capacity and the sun already climbing high into the sky I was ready to assert myself. In the hush I went for the safe one. It was safe all right, but the result was a disappointing 49 ft 3¾ in. Disappointing, that is, compared with the distances I had been achieving in recent training.

The second one I really let go. When the figures came up on the track scoreboard at the metric equivalent of 53 ft 1¾ in I knew that it was the best I had ever achieved in a pentathlon. Even so I felt faintly disappointed again. This was where I had to put some distance between myself and those I knew to be my real rivals. Rosendahl I knew all about but Pollak I had never even set eyes on before coming to Munich. I can remember the feeling of relief when she turned out to be somewhat smaller, physically, than she appeared in her photographs, but for all that I had a very genuine respect for her record and was apprehensive about her potential.

Before my third put I heard one of the many photographers talking to me in English. For some reason I had assumed they were all Germans in the centre of the arena, but this was Peter Kemp of the Associated Press, and I was so cheered up by it that I said, 'Watch this, it's going to be a new British record.' It wasn't. My third and last throw hadn't improved on my second but I had no reason to be disheartened. That second throw had beaten the field.

It put me in the lead of the pentathlon with 1920 points. Pollak, some six inches behind me in the shot, had now moved into second place with 1879. Heide Rosendahl hadn't profited greatly from her extra warm-up time for her best distance with the shot was 45 ft 5¾ in. She was now lying third overall with 1783 points but I knew, West Germany knew and everyone who knew anything about athletics anywhere in the world knew, that she still had her best events to come.

But as we gathered up our belongings and left the track for lunch and the long wait for the single event of the afternoon, the high jump, I also knew that I had never been in a better mental state in any major competition. After all the upsets, the suspicions, the cat-and-mouse games of the previous few hours I should, by nature, have been a sack of nerves. Unaccountably the fuss over my placing in the second heat of the hurdles, the non-arrival of the car that was due to take us to the stadium, the near-disaster over my shoes and the gamesmanship the Germans had employed to give their own competitors an unfair advantage had served only to put me in a militant mood and give me more confidence than I had known before. For one thing, I could see a marked change in the attitude of the German track officials towards me. That didn't do any harm. Furthermore, I had at last come face to face with Pollak, whom I'd never met in competition before. Throughout the year she had been steadily rising as the new young star in the firmament and as we charted her achievements, back in Belfast, we had grown more and more concerned. What is more, every magazine and newspaper photograph I had ever seen of her made her look like some massive Amazon, some towering Brünhilde. In the flesh she turned out to be quite moderately built and the very sight of her broke down a big psychological barrier.

The wait for the third event of the day, the high jump, was interminable. We had finished the shot by midday and were not due back to resume the battle before five o'clock. The success of the morning, however, had worked wonders with my digestive juices. Unfortunately, having decided to stay at the stadium, we discovered there was no food for the athletes. We compromised with fruit and chocolate from a stall and joined Ted Chappell, the team physiotherapist in the warm-up arena. Then for a couple of hours I lay down, utterly relaxed. When the call came and I gathered up a fresh set of clothes it no longer felt like walking out into Death Row. I bounced out, eager for the fight, and the mood endured out there in the stadium as the sun went down and a small chill came into the air and the evening turned into something very close to fantasy.

My previous best personal performances in the high jump were

5 ft 6 in for the pentathlon and 5 ft 10¼ in for straight competition.
I knew that 5 ft 6 in would not be good enough in this company and
my first four jumps, with the bar steadily going up to that mark
from 5 ft 1 in, presented no problems. I was over, clear, each time
with the new Fosbury flop technique which I had adopted the
previous year. But then, at 5 ft 7¼ in, I ran into real trouble. Twice
I tried and twice I felt the bar go off beneath me. It left me with just
one attempt and a lot of unfulfilled ambition and it was now that
an invisible, but very real, lifeline into the crowd saved me.

Coaches are barred from coming out on to the track or having
any kind of verbal contact with competitors. But, there, fifty
yards away in the lower part of the stand, was Buster. He was
wearing, as always, the bright yellow anorak which he used so
that I could pick him out immediately in the crowd. I never had to
look far. Without fail, wherever I happened to be in the arena or
whatever competition was in progress, Buster was at the closest
possible point permitted by the rules. How he did it I shall never
know for I don't think he ever bought a ticket throughout the whole
Olympics. Anyway a ticket placing him a hundred rows back at the
far end of that gigantic grandstand would have been useless. Buster
used his wits and his driving personality instead. He was a hustler,
and although that Olympic Stadium was under the greatest security
guard ever flung over a sporting event he hustled his way to any
point he wanted. He was a well-built man and when his face was
set with those determined lines I suspect that any steward or
attendant would have been unwise to stop him.

But there he was, exactly where and when I so desperately needed
him. He was standing on his seat pumping his arms to indicate that
I must run harder into the bar and then performing a kind of
exaggerated mark-time, rather like some guardsman, to demonstrate
that I should get my knees up higher. At the previous Commonwealth Games, when I had got into a hopeless muddle with my run
in the long jump, I had panicked. Now, when some small sense of
panic was almost justified, I was quite calm. It can be quite uncanny,
this relationship between coach and athlete, but his confidence
flooded into me. He knew every thought and doubt that had been
going through my mind and it was suddenly as though his brain had
been supplanted into mine. I ran in hard for that critical third jump
at 5 ft 7¼ in, got my knees up higher and sailed over.

My chances would have perished then and there had I failed, but now the whole of my body was alive. Buster wanted to keep it that way, too. He gave me a thumbs-up and waved his arms, ordering me to keep sprinting up and down the track, warming up for every jump.

The bar went up to 5 ft $8\frac{1}{2}$ in and I was over first time. It moved up to 5 ft $9\frac{1}{4}$ in, now only fractionally below the best height I had ever achieved. Again a minor crisis here, with two failures, but once more the third and final jump was a perfect one. It had a liberating effect which is impossible to describe. Nothing felt beyond me and when they moved it up to 5 ft 10 in I was over again, first time, to equal a personal record which had been achieved in very different circumstances. Not only that: it was this jump which killed off the opposition. No-one else got over. I was now alone, leaping into the unknown.

There are many scenes which an athlete who has known some success will carry to the grave. For me the scene which followed will remain the most vivid of all for I came out of my intense concentration for a moment to realise an extraordinary thing. The great crowd were still in their seats but there were now only two athletes still competing in the whole of that space-age coliseum. At the far end Wolfgang Nordwig, a young engineer from Leipzig, was the sole survivor in the men's pole vault. He was climbing into the sky, again and again, in pursuit of an Olympic record. At my end there was only Mary P, as alone on the stage as a singer left behind by the choir. The floodlights were on and looking outwards from that almost Wagnerian setting I could see masses of waving Union Jacks and hear the crowd chanting my name again and again. It is not being modest to say it all felt like some dream for there had been occasions in the past when I had completed a pentathlon high jump without a solitary spectator in sight and then, by the time I had showered and changed, had to clamber over a wall to get out of an already-locked stadium. Now some fifty thousand had stayed behind to see *me* and were shouting *my* name just as they shouted the names of entire football teams at a Wembley Cup Final. Behind me, too, I knew that Buster and Marea were wildly urging me on. It was all so unreal that at times I felt disembodied, almost as though I were up there in the stands watching myself.

At the other end Wolfgang Nordwig must have been experiencing much the same sensation for when I jumped he stood aside and waited and when he vaulted I stood aside and watched him clear another mark and joined in the great explosion of East German applause. Then it would be my turn again and I would settle down, shake all the other thoughts out of my head and begin to run.

I have never been so emotionally involved with a crowd. I so badly wanted to give them back some of the love and encouragement they were giving me that I found myself doing incredible, extrovert things that had never entered my head before. I was coming out of the pit and then kicking up my heels like a foal. I was running down to the edge of the track to blow kisses to one particularly noisy group of British spectators. Each time the tears were welling up in my eyes until all I could see of them was a watery blur. I have seen it all on television films many times since and, each time, I simply cannot believe it is me. For all my extrovert antics as a front garden skipper back in my childhood days in Liverpool it was all completely out of character. It was Sheila Sherwood who said afterwards: 'Christ, after *that* you'll have no trouble getting on the Morecambe and Wise Show. You loved them all.'

Some day, when science knows even more about adrenalin, it may all be explained. For me, at the end of a day of enormous tension and physical strain, an overwhelming desire to give more and more for my coach and my team manager and those marvellous supporters who had come half way across Europe was pushing me onwards and upwards.

The bar went up to 5 ft $10\frac{3}{4}$ in. Over first time. It moved on again to 5 ft $11\frac{1}{2}$ in, now $5\frac{1}{2}$ in higher than I had achieved only a year before. Again, up and over first time.

It had to end somewhere and it did, at 6 ft $0\frac{1}{2}$ in. Even then, in that electrifying atmosphere, I almost made it with the second of my three final attempts. It was only the great long-drawn 'Oooh' when the bar fell for the third time that broke the spell. There were still two events and a bitter struggle to come on the morrow but I knew then, as I stood there, that I had been privileged to experience to the very depths of my emotions the meaning of two lines written by a gentleman named Thomas Osbert Mordaunt. 'One crowded hour of glorious life,' he said, 'is worth an age without a name.' By God, how right he was.

10. The Long Wait

When Mary Peters finally disappeared from public view that evening she walked into a high-ceilinged tunnel at the end of the stadium and a situation which nice ladies never discuss. Inevitably she was besieged by autograph hunters. One hand which came out of the crowd proffered a piece of official looking paper which Mary accepted and started to sign. 'Nein,' said a lady in a white coat, 'come with me, please.'

Mary was then led into an ante-room with a lavatory cabinet built into the corner. The door was open. It had to remain open while she had to produce a urine sample into a jug to prove that she had not been under the influence of artificial stimulants while high-jumping as she had never high-jumped before. Other athletes, hospital patients and military personnel can testify to the fact that peeing to order can occasionally make Euclid seem child's play. The lady in the white coat turned all the taps on to facilitate this natural function but it was fully fifteen minutes before Mary was able to comply and join a jubilant Buster and Marea outside. By then the sample had been transferred to two bottles, each bearing a number which Mary had chosen at random, corked with corks which she had signed, further secured by two strips of adhesive tape, also signed, and finally protected against all forms of tampering by the application of two caps of freshly melted sealing wax. These were for immediate dispatch to two independent analysts.

This procedure may well sound a tiresome intrusion after appearing all day before 80 000 spectators inside a stadium and a further 400 million on television but Mary complied willingly. Nothing was ever heard of the samples again, thus confirming that the hurdles, the shot-put and the high jump had all been Mary's own work and owed nothing to drugs. This has not always been the case at major sporting events and is one of the reasons why Mary submitted to the whole examination with equanimity and good humour.

I was less tired than if I had done a day's Christmas shopping in
Oxford Street. The euphoria of it all kept me up there in the clouds
and as I walked out of the stadium all I wanted to do was go back
to the Village and watch the re-run of the day's other athletics on
television. Buster and Marea were over the moon and they took me
along to the Puma shop, which didn't sell pumas but athletics'
equipment made by the German firm using that trade-name. I
can't say that much of what I was watching registered. The agony
of waiting had not yet hit me and nor had the realisation that not
only was I within twenty-four hours of the greatest goal that an
athlete can achieve but also exactly the same time away from
incalculable disappointment. Certainly I was ahead after three
events, but the knowledge that Rosendahl's two favourite events –
the long jump and the 200 metres – were yet to be tackled came as
a sobering reminder that chickens are not to be counted. Rosendahl
had had a bad afternoon. Like me she had tried to adapt the flop
method of high-jumping but it had not worked out for her. She
reverted to the old Corinthian style of the straddle-jump, where you
go over on your back instead of your front, and had achieved only
5 ft 5 in. Pollak, however, had used the flop technique as well and
achieved a personal best of 5 ft 9¼ in. We were therefore going to bed
with me leading on 2969 points, Pollak second on 2872 points and
Rosendahl lying fifth with 2668. Between Pollak and Rosendahl
came Valentina Tikhomirova, with whom I was shortly destined to
have what may be described as a small contretemps, and the
youthful Christine Bodner, who had been such an unconscious
help in the hurdles. Tikhomirova was third with 2744 points and
Bodner fourth with 2709. Both were and are fine athletes but I still
felt I could dismiss them from my mind. Pollak I could by no means
discount as yet. She might be smaller than I had imagined from her
photographs but she was a dangerously wonderful performer. As for
Rosendahl, I had nothing but respect. She was tough, she was hard,
she was a brilliant long-jumper and a terrific sprinter. And she was
West German. My own experience of that very afternoon had confirmed for me, if confirmation were needed, how a crowd can lift
one and she, of course, would strive in front of an adoring mass who
wanted nothing more than for her achievements to be rewarded by
a rendering of a national anthem which the British know as a hymn.
It was the same hymn to which Princess Anne, a little more than a

year later, was to walk down the aisle of Westminster Abbey: *Glorious Things of Thee Are Spoken*. The words, in German, have an altogether different connotation and I was not prepared to dwell on them as I sat there in that shop.

Buster had what seemed a million sheets of paper with ten million permutations scrawled across them. If Rosendahl did *that* then this was what I must do in time or distance. If Rosendahl did *this* then that was what I had to achieve. He had calculated everything. My only job was to jump and run. I wasn't going to win either of the second day's events. That I knew. What I had to do was keep in touch, maintain my overall lead. The figures started spinning round in my head and I absorbed less and less of what was appearing on the television screen.

There was a sharp tap on the window. A young man with a beard was peering in. He grinned, stuck his thumbs up and mouthed the words 'Good Luck.' It was David Bedford. I was almost a veteran by the time he had arrived in athletics and had never exchanged a word with him. He had soon established a reputation of being a raving egocentric and only that morning had given an interview to a London newspaper advising every man, woman and child in the country to watch him the following day as he proposed to run the legs off the world in the 10 000 metres final. This kind of personal propaganda did not endear him to everyone but I liked his gesture. He had his own pressures and problems at that moment, but he had time to concern himself with mine. I appreciated that very much.

We sat there for an hour or more before I could think about going to bed. I was very happy. I was tense but I wasn't nervous, which is where we came in at the prologue to these recollections. That long, that dreadfully long, lone night lay ahead. I tossed and I turned and I turned and I tossed. I went back over every moment of that day and tried to imagine tomorrow. Sound sleep was impossible. I occasionally picked up *Time* magazine but the words were meaningless. One figure kept roaring through my brain: 19·6.

Nineteen feet six inches was what the shrewd Buster McShane had calculated Mary had to achieve in the long jump, the penultimate event of the pentathlon, if she was to be there with a big chance of winning the gold medal. Even if Rosendahl leaped close to a world record, which he considered unlikely after the sapping strain of the previous day's events.

*he believed Mary could still be in touch when it came to the final event,
the 200 metres, which Rosendahl was surely going to win. It is quite
impossible for the layman to attempt to follow Buster's myriad calculations. Mary herself couldn't. Very few sportswriters, except the most
diligent athletics specialists, could keep up with him. There were two
events to go, three contestants there with a chance, two more lurking in
the wings and that unpredictable fellow, fate, to feed into computers. It
added up to too many imponderables. Most of us, even the spectacularly
irreligious, said a small prayer and fell soundly asleep. We were back
in the stadium well before the appointed hour of eleven o'clock on that
Sunday morning. We were anxious to see what she looked like, what
shape she was in. We saw only what her opponents saw which was a
radiant girl, smiling and gleaming with confidence, and if anyone had
told you she had not slept a wink you would have called him a fool,
a defeatist and a downright liar.*

If my performance during the closing stages of the high jump the
previous evening had been out of character I was, that Sunday
morning, quite unrecognisable even to myself. The lasting criticism
of me throughout my career had been that I had concerned myself
too often with the welfare of the losers. I had been a ready shoulder
to cry on. Now I was thinking of no one but myself. It is not with a
great deal of pride that I now recall that during our warm-up on the
outdoor track that morning I used Ann Wilson, my own team
colleague, quite mercilessly for my own purposes. We were good
friends and remain so, but she had not done well and she wasn't
going to win a medal or get anywhere near one. All my generosity
had gone and since she was a very good long-jumper I joined her
in practice and, unknowingly to her, got her to raise my own
performance. I was beating her off short approaches and it boosted
my confidence enormously. I simply didn't care what it did to her.

Back in the stadium, with the jumping about to start, there was
another small incident which illustrates my mood and the general
cut-throat atmosphere. Valentina Tikhomirova, the Russian girl
who had been European champion back in 1966, kept brushing
against me every time she passed. You're not exactly cramped for
space out there on the track so I could only assume that she was
doing it deliberately to unnerve and irritate me. Clearly she thought
she was still in with a chance, particularly if she could drive me up

the wall and make me lose concentration. It had to stop. The next time she did it I drove an elbow into her ribs, quite violently, and kept walking as though nothing had happened. Out of the corner of my eye I could see her limp away. It never happened again and I knew I had won that little struggle of wills quite easily.

Again, as in the shot, you only get three attempts in the pentathlon long jump so it is an enormous boost if you can get a big one in first time. I measured out my run of 112 feet, which is eaten up in eighteen strides when you're travelling in the opposite direction, and put down Larry as my marker. Larry is a small leprechaun who'd been given to me by a girl friend at London Airport on the way out to the Games. The German officials either didn't like the look of him or else suspected that the Irish little people really do have supernatural powers. They ordered me to move him and use a conventional marker instead. I sat him back on the grass where he still had a good view and proceeded to pull out, at the first attempt, the biggest jump of my life. It was certainly over 20 ft, hugely past the 19 ft 6 in which Buster had calculated as being absolutely necessary. Unfortunately it was a foul. By the smallest fraction of an inch I had over-stepped the board.

Once more it was a crisis moment, but yet again the presence of Buster, in his yellow anorak, forced back the wave of panic. He was on his feet in the stands, smiling, and his thumbs were up. It was the only gesture he made. It was just as well for I was soon in need of every ounce of confidence I could get. To a great explosion of a roar from a crowd which was already back at its capacity 80 000 Rosendahl hurdled herself into a phenomenal leap of 22 ft 5 in, a mere quarter of an inch short of her world record. To produce it under the extreme pressure some thirty-nine hours into a pentathlon was a prodigious feat. It was certainly more than Buster had ever expected from her in his calculations and, of course, it drew her right back among the front-runners in the overall fight. I was always going to give ground to her here but to have to give *that* much ground didn't have much to commend itself to my nervous system.

My second jump was safe, in terms that I didn't overstep this time, but it wasn't long enough: 19 ft 4¼ in. The third one, by my personal standards, was a beauty but it led to an agonised wait while the officials examined the board for a foul, then called up the chief judge from miles away for a final ruling. Eventually he stood up straight and signalled that it was legal. At 19 ft 7½ in it was almost exactly what Buster had demanded of me but the mathematics had been thrown out once more by Rosendahl's jump, which was fully six inches better than we'd anticipated.

Mercifully Rosendahl couldn't improve on that in her remaining jumps. But in the meantime Pollak had put the pressure on, too, with a jump of 20 ft 4½ in. It meant that the three of us were now almost deadlocked, with me just ahead with 3871 points, Pollak closed up on 3824 points and Rosendahl right back in the running in third place with 3750. There was only the 200 metres sprint to come.

It was a dangerous moment to start revealing one's admiration for opponents but Heide Rosendahl deserved it. I had known her for five years and her career, at the highest level, had been pursued by ill-luck. She had been deprived of a medal at the European Games in Athens when the entire West German team withdrew for political reasons. At the Mexico Olympics, where she had been clear favourite to win the gold, she pulled a muscle warming-up on the opening morning and a year's intense preparation had been laid to waste in a second. In Mexico, as in Munich, I had asked 'Where is Rosendahl?' Then it was her colleague Ingrid Becker who shrugged, gave an odd little smile and just said 'She's out.' Becker knew that she could now win the gold herself and she did precisely that.

Now, four years later, here was Heide going for her life. It was almost as though all those years of frustration had driven her to that superhuman jump. To the mass of German spectators it was charging the climax to the pentathlon with even more emotion. I could well have done without it. Between the events John Le Masurier had been filling the West German coaches up with all sorts of fictitious details about the times and distances I was capable of, but the hour of kidology was over. Now a split second over 200 metres would decide it.

Towards the end of the long jump I heard someone urgently calling me from the photographers' trench alongside the track. It was another friend, Mel Watman, editor of the small but authoritative magazine, *Athletics Weekly*. He, like Buster, had done some light-ning calculations after my final jump to work out what time I must

now achieve in the 200 metres to win the gold. He was in a high
state of excitement but I was terrified to turn round and talk to him.
Some of the other girls were still jumping and I had the dreadful
thought that I could still be disqualified for receiving trackside
'coaching.' I wasn't going to be caught like that. I was dying to talk
to Mel, to know the best or the worst, but I stayed there until the
last girl had jumped and was out of the pit.

Now came the most awful wait of all and to make it worse I lost
Buster. I assumed he would be waiting for me just outside the
athletes' entrance, but he wasn't. For twenty minutes I stood on the
grassy bank, watching car after bus pull away, taking my rivals back
to rest and sleep. There was still no sign of Buster. He had gone
away to search for a friend of ours from Bermuda but I didn't know
that at the time. All I knew was that I was being surrounded by
more and more autograph-hunters and people wanting to know how
I now considered my chances. Normally I am never abrupt with
people like that. They mean well and they are the people who keep
athletics going but at that moment I just couldn't cope. I found
myself getting more and more worked up and distressed. The pressure was really telling. I had to get out so, without making any
contact with Buster, I went back to the Village again, ate down some
yoghurt very quickly and went to my room. Janet Simpson asked me
if I wanted to be alone. I didn't, so Janet stayed with me. I was in
tears, sobbing because of emotions that I couldn't even define. I had
missed Buster's assurances when I needed them most. I was worried
that he would be angry with me for leaving the stadium without him.
I was angry at the chaos at the very moment when I needed peace.
Analysed at this distance they were all symptoms of fear. I was
afraid that I wasn't going to run as well as I could. And how I had
to run, if I were still to win: better than I had ever run in my life.

Several of my team colleagues came into my room to comfort me.
They kept saying things like 'What are you worried about? You're
certain of a medal anyway.' I kept saying, '*Any* medal's no good.
It's got to be the gold.' I could find no consolation at all in the
thought that I only had to stay alive till tea-time to become a *medal*
winner. It was gold or nothing.

The wait was terrible. Pat Cropper helped by leaving our women's
quarters, going back to the stadium, searching high and low until
she'd found Buster, complete with Bermudan friend, and telephoning

back to my room that everything was okay. It was so okay that to this day I cannot remember leaving the Village and returning to the track. I must have been in a total daze because all I recall now is getting to the entrance and seeing Buster there. He ignored the subject of how we had missed one another after the long jump. It might never have happened. He was utterly calm. All he kept saying, very softly, was 'It's all right, P, we can do it.'

His calculations about the time I had to do agreed, frighteningly, with Mel Watman's. It simply had to be the fastest I'd ever run. He didn't confuse me with figures and decimal points. I had to stay fairly close to Pollak but, more critically, I had to keep in touch with Rosendahl. Both, we knew, were going to beat me but what now was to decide it all was by how little, not how much. The respective fastest times we had ever done were 23·8 by Pollak, 23·1 by Rosendahl and 24·2 by me.

Merely hearing Buster talk about it as though it were some abstract problem in a Christmas puzzle book had the usual calming influence. But, again, that was all undone. I warmed up in the indoor track to be ready exactly at the appointed time of five minutes to five. I was then informed I would not be running until twenty minutes past. I must have looked like some poor wretch on the gallows who'd been told that he'd have to wait around for half an hour while Mr Pierpoint had his breakfast. My mind was screaming, 'I can't go on like this any longer. I've got to go now, now, now.' But Buster said, 'Just go and lie over there' and I did and my mind went totally blank until he came for me and led me across the road and into that pentathlon for the fifth and last time. He said, 'Right, P, this is it. Go.' It sounds like some rather predictable line from a film script now but at the time it was rather apt.

I walked in and alongside the trench with its hundreds of photographers and, behind them, the one hundred and twenty rows of journalists. I carried on round to the back straight where I tried a few starts and then opened up my stride for a few yards. I was aware now that while there was no one on earth who could help me any more at least my tension was being shared. The television cameras were all on this event and I knew that back home in Northern Ireland they would all be looking in: Catholics and Protestants, friends in the gym, fellow athletes and old school colleagues and Kenny McClelland, my first real coach, and Mr Woodman who,

like me, had no Irish blood in him but loved the place to distraction.
I couldn't let them down. I was running for them and Belfast now,
and that was the last thought I had before turning and going to the
starting line at the top end of the stadium with the left-hand curve
just ahead and the finishing line away down there on the horizon.

I set my blocks and practised another start or two. It wasn't right.
One of the pins clamping the blocks into the track was loose. I set
it again. There were seven of us in this final heat and nobody spoke.
I was in lane three with Bodner on the kerb, Pollak immediately to
my left, Anghelova of Bulgaria immediately on the right. Then
moving outwards were Tikhomirova, who hadn't given me any more
trouble since our 'accidental' collision, then Heide Rosendahl, then
Karen Mack.

The pistol fired and we ran.

It is impossible for me to give an objective account of the race.
There are certain athletes who claim that pressure heightens the
perception to such a degree that they see everything as though it is
happening in slow motion. I am not one of them. My recollections
are of emotions, not sights. First came the surging relief that comes
from knowing you have made a terrific start. I simply hurled myself
into the bend and flew past Anghelova, on my right, which was an
enormous boost. Around eighty metres I knew I was fractionally
up on Pollak and was still within three metres of Rosendahl, who
was going like the wind. But then, about seventy metres out I paid
for it. It was as though someone had thrown a switch and cut the
power off. All the strength drained out of me and it suddenly felt
as if my legs had turned to lead. I could sense my body getting
more and more upright, which means disaster, and it was then, in
the rising panic, that Buster's endless, driving coaching paid off.
A million times in lonely training sessions I had heard him yell
'Arms, arms' and those words now flooded my brain. I pumped
harder and harder with the arms until they were virtually dragging
my legs behind them and thus it was, with the stadium swaying
around me, that I covered those remaining metres and hit the line.
I was absolutely out.

I knew, instinctively, that I had beaten Pollak. I was so close behind her that with each tenth of a second costing ten points she
couldn't possibly catch me in the overall scoring. But what of
Rosendahl? She had run supremely well. She had opened up a gap

and kept it but was it enough to beat me out of the gold? Now only the scoreboard would tell.

I have written repeatedly of agonising waits. None was so agonising as this final one. I was standing there, engulfed by friends and rivals, staring at the scoreboard and waiting for the times that seemed stubbornly determined to remain the best kept secret of the year. Then Rosendahl's flashed up: 22·96 seconds. It was a breath-taking effort, not only the fastest she had ever run but even faster than Buster had calculated for her in his most pessimistic moment. Now all that remained was for my own time to go up there in lights. When it came – 24·08 seconds – my mind refused to understand it. For me, too, it was the fastest I had ever run, faster even than the 24·2 which I had seen as my absolute limit. But what did it mean? Had I won or lost? Were these two days and nights of physical effort and nervous exhaustion to end with the solemn playing of *Deutschland, Deutschland Uber Alles*? I couldn't work it out. I couldn't do the maths. Not even a simple subtraction.

Then someone came and put an arm round me. I turned and saw that it was Heide Rosendahl and she had the answer written in her face. The gold medal was on its way to Belfast.

A few additional facts may not come amiss to the layman. Mary finally won her gold medal by one tenth of a second. In four of her five events in Munich she established personal bests. Her final total of 4801 points was a new world and Olympic record. Miss Rosendahl finished with 4791 points, Miss Pollak with 4768. Ann Wilson, of Great Britain, finished thirteenth with 4279 points.

In Portadown, Northern Ireland, it was the last Sunday before the new school term. Donald J. Woodman, diligent headmaster, was bent low in concentration over a large and complex chart on his study desk. He was utterly absorbed. He looked up in some annoyance as a neighbour rapped on his window. 'Switch on quickly, Mary could win a gold medal,' shouted the neighbour. 'I can't stop now,' replied Donald Woodman, with his finger over the fifth-year Latin programme, 'I'm doing the timetables for next term.' Typically he completed his work before crossing the hall to his sitting-room. He was just in time to see his former head girl receive her gold medal as the greatest all-round woman athlete on either side of Christendom. 'I simply stood there,' he now recalls, 'and cried with pride.'

11. The Aftermath

Back in Munich Mary and her coach had been crying too. As soon as the result was known Mary ran towards the tunnel where, win or lose, she had arranged to meet Buster McShane. She was besieged by reporters grappling for instant interviews. Then Buster arrived and she broke off, leaving microphones prodding the empty air. They stood there, arms locked around one another, with tears flowing down their faces. For once the press were guilty of intrusion into private joy. That struggle was over. But it may occur to some that living with triumph is not exactly child's play either.

No one on earth could have understood the emotions we felt at that moment. They cannot be described. For a few seconds no one else existed, but then we were both caught up again in the sheer chaos of it all. One voice, however, caught me totally unawares. 'Did you know, Mary,' said John Goodbody, the athletics writer of the London *Evening News*, 'that your father has been watching you all day?' Had it been Chairman Mao or a reincarnated Gandhi I could not have been more surprised. I had last seen my father two and a half years earlier when he decided to live in Australia. I had last heard of him on holiday in Canada. I knew it couldn't be true. Buster, thinking quickly as always, showed a little apprehension. He took Goodbody aside and asked for a full description. It was as well to do that if you came from Northern Ireland. But the man described could have been no one but my father. Swearing everyone to secrecy, telling none of my aunts or uncles in case word got out, he had joined a party of Australian businessmen and come half way round the world to see me win. That I could lose had apparently never occurred to him. I could almost understand his innocence. He had never seen me compete in a major championship before.

I was desperate to run and find him then and there but that is easier said than done when you are caught up in the tailwind of an Olympic victory.

For a start you do not just go and collect your medal. You have to be prepared for it as thoroughly as if you were appearing on the set of some American musical. On the way back along the track verge to meet the make-up artist and the hairdresser I saw Arthur Gold in the stand, unzipped the top of my track suit and thrust out the figures '111' which were still pinned to my front. It was his choice of omen and he shared the joke but it was the last unladylike gesture I was to be permitted for quite some time. In the make-up room where they doll you up to appear before a television audience usually quoted as four hundred million it was tensely serious. In the hands of the male German hairdresser I felt like Madame Pompadour getting ready for a night out with the lads. He drew my hair back tightly and used about a hundred pins and clips to weave it into the most elaborate style. I didn't like it but felt a little timid about disturbing such a great artist at work. Buster, when he came down to see what was happening, had no such inhibitions. 'My God, P,' he said, 'what the hell have they done to your hair? Get those pins out right away.' We stood by the side of the track pulling out pin after pin and clip after clip until I was able to shake my hair free and feel myself again. Armande of Munich, or whatever he called himself, was mortified at our wanton destruction but Buster was right.

We had a long wait in that make-up room before the medal ceremony. Heide Rosendahl and Burglinde Pollak were there. We didn't talk but Heide handed me a cigarette. I was almost relieved to see that she smoked as well. Somehow she was sharing my guilt. I urge young people not to start this stupid habit and can testify to the fact that I would have been a better athlete had I never smoked. But we are dealing in the truth here and the fact is that I got through an entire packet of cigarettes during the pentathlon. I guessed, looking at Heide, that she'd probably done the same. The strain of all that waiting hadn't been my exclusive problem. Even now the waiting wasn't done with. I desperately wanted to dash away and see Daddy and fling my arms round all my friends, but the Germans had laid down strict instructions about the protocol of medal-presentation ceremonies. Nobody went anywhere until they were over.

But they certainly weren't going to stop me going out to the track-side to watch David Bedford's race. David, of course, had alerted the world to sit by their television sets and watch him win for Britain, and word of it must have reached 10 Downing Street. There, high up in the VIP box alongside Herr Willi Brandt and Princess Grace of Monaco, was the British Prime Minister, Edward Heath. Apparently he'd arrived just before my 200 metres. I was desperately disappointed when David didn't win his race. I suspect that that was what the Prime Minister had come to see but at least he had had the consolation of witnessing one gold medal won for Britain. As it turned out, it was the only British athletics gold of the Games.

I was about to go back into the waiting-room when someone said, 'Mr Heath would like to see you.' I went and found Buster because I wanted him to be there as well, and then Mr Heath came down the endless steps from the VIP gallery. He was very jolly and charming and kind and I rather got the impression he was a little surprised to have discovered that there was actually another Briton competing that day. We chatted away for a few minutes and I found myself telling him what all the time had been uppermost in my mind. 'At last,' I said, 'there's some good news for Northern Ireland.' He smiled and said, 'Yes, I just hope they don't celebrate too much in Belfast tonight.' I am very glad, in retrospect, that Buster was present at that conversation although the reason why won't become obvious to the reader for another page or two.

There was still another delay before the medal ceremony because the last lap of the walk was in progress. But at last the moment came and Heide, Burglinde and I were assembled in the correct order to walk out into the centre of the arena for the supreme moment of any athlete's life. There has in recent years been much controversy about the raising of flags and the playing of national anthems at the Olympics. The anti-argument is that it all perpetuates nationalism and nationalistic attitudes which have no place in events like the Olympics which profess to unite, not divide, the youth of the world. All I can say is that the people who put forward that view all seem to have one thing in common: they haven't actually prepared themselves for four years to run for their countries. I was very proud and very emotional to be walking out there to receive a medal for the people of Northern Ireland.

I felt certain the tears would be streaming down my face the moment Lord Exeter had slipped the medal collar over my head and they began to play *God Save the Queen*. Doubtless they would have done but for the disturbance down on my left as we faced the flags. Poor Burglinde Pollak was gasping and sobbing and almost choking and I was so concerned about her that my own tears held back throughout the unforgettable moments when the slow, solemn notes filled that towering stadium and the only movement seemed to be the Union Jack rising slowly to the masthead. These are the moments when your mind floods with visions of the green hills and familiar streets of home and yet I stood there worrying about why Burglinde was crying. Was it because she hadn't won for East Germany, a country whose sporting system puts such a high premium on winning? The language barrier prevented me from asking her but Heide assured me, as we walked back across the track, that this wasn't so. Heide found it hard to conceal her disappointment but Burglinde was simply overwhelmed, it seemed, at having won the bronze medal.

It was about then that the whole roof fell in. I wanted to race away and find my father, wherever he was, but that was impossible. I now fell into the hands of the communications industry whose competitive instincts make anything that happens out on the track seem as gentle as evensong. The BBC, ITV and ITN all wanted interviews at once. So did every radio interviewer who had a single listener who could understand English. And all the while there was a somewhat officious and extremely agitated German trying to drag me away to a room down in the bowels of the stadium where the writing-Press were waiting. 'You must come immediately,' he kept saying, but I'd had enough of being herded around like some prize-winning exhibit at Smithfields. Mark Andrews, of Independent Television News, turned on the official and made the only intelligent suggestion put forward so far. 'We'll let the lady decide,' he said. I knew I could see all the English writers later so I decided to do the television interviews first.

The ITV men had first use of the studio, if that is the right word for the cramped areas in which those armies of technicians and journalists and front men had to work. I was greeted by a beaming Dickie Davies clutching two bottles of champagne. We drank one there and then before the BBC interviews started. I was still being pursued by the German official who made yet another counter-attack and another furious argument broke out. 'She's ours.' 'Nein, she is not.' 'Yes, she is.' 'She is not. It is very rude what is happening here.' Certain other remarks followed this which I have no intention of repeating here. Anyway, I was very relaxed. I'd just won a gold medal.

From the moment the BBC people took over the studio I sensed that something curious was happening. Chris Brasher was the interviewer and he sat directly in front of me with Buster at my side. Suddenly, mid-way through the interview, I was astonished to see Buster getting up from his chair. I couldn't work it out. We talked on for another few moments and then I noticed that someone else was taking his seat in the chair beside me. I turned and came face to face with my father for the first time since he had emigrated to Australia.

Anyone who saw that reunion on television will have a better idea than I have about what went on. My father had sworn the whole family to secrecy about his visit to Munich. He just turned up, convinced his only daughter was going to win the gold medal, and introduced himself that morning to the BBC staff. Since the whole place was guarded like the Crown Jewels they asked him how on earth he had got into the TV offices. Apparently my father drew himself up to his full height and delivered himself of probably the most portentious sentence he has ever spoken: 'Young man, it is not for nothing that I have been in the insurance business all my life.'

It was wonderful to see him. I was very excited but no more excited than my father who, it seems, had been telling everyone for months that I was going to win. Heavens, was he proud, this man who years before had taken us to sports stores in Northern Ireland to buy us equipment he really couldn't afford. In the end I felt quite sorry for Chris Brasher. Chris is an excellent interviewer of athletes because of his deep understanding of the sport but here was an occasion when he was hard-pressed to get a question in edgeways. My father just wouldn't stop talking.

Eventually it was over and my father, Buster and myself placed ourselves at the disposal of the German official who by now had almost given up hope of ever getting us to the Press conference. I was still carrying the other bottle of ITV's champagne which we opened on the rostrum and shared with Heide and Burglinde. This helped because what followed was a terrible bore. Every question was ponderously translated into three languages and by the time they'd finished that you'd forgotten what the questioner was asking. Then, when you had finished your answer, that, too, was translated three times. It seemed a fairly pointless exercise when some of the questions were as profound as 'How old are you?' or 'Did you think you would win?' You soon learn that the good reporters very rarely ask questions at these kind of conferences. If they have an intelligent question and you are prepared to give a reasonably intelligent answer why should they waste it all filling the notebooks of those who just sit there and wait for it to fall into their laps?

By the time it was all over I was rearing to go on the evening's celebrations, but first the three medal winners had to go to a drug test. This was somewhat more cursory than the previous day's and also, I thought, somewhat belated. The medals had been awarded. It was soon established that no grave suspicion hung over anyone and so I went back and found Dickie Davies who had promised to run me back to the Village. The winding-down process is important because, suddenly, there is a huge void in your life. It is all over, for better or for worse, and now there is no demanding target consuming every waking second of your life. I wanted to get out on the town with my close friends but it wasn't quite as easy as that. First of all my father, in his excitement, had lost his coat, his hat and his briefcase. Some German officials assured him that they would find them and return them to him tomorrow, but I knew that wouldn't satisfy him. 'I'm not leaving here until I've got them,' he said, and of course, he didn't. We found them in the end.

All I wanted to do then was slip into the Village, change into some evening clothes and leave. It wasn't that easy. Getting back into Room 857 in Block B was about as simple as getting out of Colditz a few years previously. The whole corridor was strewn with flowers and there were toilet paper garlands stretched from door-handle to door-handle all the way down to my room. When I finally got to my door all the girls in the British team had written their congratulations around it on the wall. Inside there were still more flowers and the telegrams were beginning to pile up. Almost the first I opened was from Mr William Whitelaw, the British Minister in charge of affairs in Northern Ireland.

By the time we got away it was time to drop my father back at the main station in Munich because he was living an hour's train journey out of town. We then went to Buster's hotel and had a few drinks as a kind of net-practice for the evening that lay ahead. By now Derek Ibbotson had arrived to drive us out to the château-like hotel the Puma sports equipment people had taken over miles outside Munich. They had arranged a party which compared pretty favourably with anything the Borgias used to set up for their more peaceful at-homes. There was enough champagne for Mark Spitz to have won seven gold medals in, and enormous amounts of food for anyone who felt inclined to eat. One thing impressed me enormously. They presented me with a watch. This was always a generous thing to do but I only discovered late in the evening that being a Sunday, they had had to go into the city and beg a jeweller to open his store so that they could buy it. Memories dimmed a little as the evening progressed but I do recall a couple of things. Derek Ibbotson's daughter sat next to me at the dining table and kept pinching the chips off my plate. And, at some point in the proceedings, I was summoned to what appeared to be the only still-connected telephone in the place. It was in the kitchen and sitting there, amid all the chaos and noise, I gave an interview to the *Belfast Telegraph*. What they printed the next morning, under the headline MARY'S GOLDEN DAY was a most beautiful piece of writing which captured every emotion I had felt down that extra-ordinary day.

It was Thomas Mann who described Munich as the incandescent city and his words fitted it exactly as we returned to the village. It may have been five a.m., or nearer six, but the dawn was certainly breaking out there over all the Russias and bathing the city in a lovely glow. I slept for two, perhaps three hours, and awoke on top of the world. There was, in any case, no chance of sleeping any longer. All the girls in the British team were crowding into my room demanding to see my medal. They'd brought more champagne and, outside the door, there was a stack of literally hundreds of tele-grams. They began helping me open them. They were from life-long friends and people I'd never heard of. They were from rich people and poor people and business organisations and household names and the accumulative effect was to make me wonder what the difference would have been had I won the silver instead of the gold. The sweat and the training and effort and the dedication and the sacrifice are precisely the same but Buster's uncompromising philosophy was right: there is no substitute for coming first. I had known enough moments of disappointment to know how to enjoy this one to the full.

It was then that two things happened which brought me back to earth.

In the evening I joined Marea Hartman and some of the British girls to attend a reception. I was in the mood for anything and everything – except what actually occurred. I had not been there very long before a gentleman of impeccable speech and manners approached me. It appeared that he was something to do with the British Government. He informed me that the Prime Minister, Mr Heath, was giving a lunch party the following day and would be delighted if I would attend. He took the trouble to add that I would be sitting at the Prime Minister's right hand. It seemed that I was to be some kind of guest of honour.

I replied that I was very honoured and, of course, I would love to attend. Naturally I added that since my coach, Buster McShane, had done as much to win my gold medal as I had, I presumed he would be receiving an invitation as well.

The gentleman took the suggestion completely in his stride and said he would go and make sure that was in order. I went away and told Marea and Sandy Duncan, secretary of the British Olympic Association, about the invitation and then waited for the Government's representative to return. Finally he did, looking, I felt, somewhat uneasy. 'Mr Heath is delighted to have you along to lunch,' he said, 'but is your coach an official member of the British Olympic party?'

I said, 'No, he isn't. He's my private coach.'

To which the reply was, 'Well, I'm awfully sorry about this, but this lunch is for members of the official party only.'

I then said, 'Well, would you kindly explain to Mr Heath that I shan't be there tomorrow.'

The gentleman was only nonplussed for a second. He said: 'Oh yes. I'll tell him you have a prior engagement.'

I answered 'No, I would rather you tell him the truth.'

That, so far as I can remember, is the exact exchange of words in this rather unusual little episode. Prime Ministers have far more important things to do with their time than listen to athletes asking if their coaches may accompany them to lunch. But after our conversation at the trackside in the Olympic Stadium the previous day I have a small suspicion that Mr Heath never received the message exactly as I delivered it. Anyway I never went to the lunch and nor do I have too many regrets if I upset the seating arrangements.

As it happened there was soon something else to occupy my mind.

What occurred next, at this same reception, has never been told before. As a British journalist covering the 1972 Munich Olympics I cannot forgive myself for being so absorbed by what was happening on the track the day after Mary won her gold medal that I did not stay at her shoulder. Had I done so I, or any of the other 4000 journalists in attendance, could scarcely have failed to learn something considerably to her disadvantage.

By the time I got back to my group after the official refusal to allow Buster to attend the Prime Minister's lunch I could feel a certain tension in the atmosphere. The light had gone out of the morning. My father and Buster had their heads together and were clearly arguing, and at my approach they broke off and went to the gents. When they returned I got hold of Buster and demanded to know what was going on. He said, 'I'll tell you later.' But that wasn't good enough. I wanted to know.

Buster looked at my father. My father looked at Buster. I stood my ground. Finally Buster said, 'All right, come over here.' We threaded our way through the little groups and the general buzz of the cocktail party and went on to the balcony outside. No one was there. Buster said, 'Look, a message has come through. It threatens that you will be shot and your flat will be blown up if you go back to Belfast.'

So that was what all the whispering had been about. That was the piece of paper Buster and my father had been looking at when I came back from my meeting with Mr Heath's representative. I didn't go cold or faint or any of the other things that happen in novels. I simply asked to see the message but Buster wouldn't show it to me.

In fact it was to be more than a year before Mary Peters was to learn the full contents of that message and the exact sequence of events that led up to her being told of a threat to her life. It began when an anonymous caller from Belfast telephoned the BBC in London and asked for a message to be passed on to her in Munich. It contained the following sentences, and I quote verbatim. My source is Mary's father who has the original note at his home in Sydney. 'Mary Peters is a Protestant and has won a medal for Britain. An attempt will be made on her life and it will be blamed on the IRA. Tell Mary Peters to say something about bringing the people together. I don't want to turn her into a martyr. Her home will be going up in the near future.' Late on the evening of September 4, 1972, this message was relayed to the BBC's Olympic headquarters in Munich. A BBC official took it straight to the British Olympic Association offices where the president, Lord Rupert Nevill, treasurer to the Duke of Edinburgh, was called in to handle the affair. At his London home, though only after receiving Mary's personal permission to discuss the matter for the preparation of this book, Lord Nevill revealed what happened next. 'Naturally,' he said, 'we immediately alerted the Special Branch at Scotland Yard. But our first concern was to keep the whole thing out of the Press, to keep it from Miss Peters and to play the whole thing down. I couldn't see that anything could be gained from Miss Peters knowing about it. I sent for her father instead and explained everything to him. Obviously security at this point was our responsibility but, at some point, the final decision about where she went after Munich was a family matter.'

They were probably doing what they thought best by bringing my father into it, but I was furious when I heard. They didn't know Daddy as well as I did. The row he and Buster had been having when I went back to join them was simply over my father insisting that I never went back to Belfast. He was very upset and emotional. Buster was completely calm. Out on the balcony he said, 'What are you going to do, P?' I said, 'This is a nut-case. There's no question about it. Of course I'm going back to Belfast.'

I am no simpleton. I knew that stranger things than this, with no warning at all, had happened in Northern Ireland. But I just didn't believe that anyone should want to kill me. What did upset me was the distressing effect it had all had on my father. All at once the euphoria had gone and everything had gone flat. The whole

British women's team were going out to another party that night,
but I couldn't face it. I made an excuse to Marea and instead joined
a small group including Buster and Janet Simpson and her fiancé
and went to dinner in Munich's big revolving restaurant. I was
conscious that I was quiet and off-colour and to explain my mood
I told Janet, in confidence, what had happened. As luck would have
it our return to the Village coincided exactly with the return of the
other British girls from their party. Those who weren't due to
compete for a couple of days, or had already completed their events,
were in spectacular form. It was pretty obvious that it hadn't been
a teetotal party. Sheila Sherwood and Della Pascoe were dancing
about and singing and when we got into the lift they pressed every
single button so that they could share at least a snatch of their song
with every single floor on the way up to our quarters where yet
another impromptu party immediately started.

All I wanted to do was get to my room, put the light out and
sleep, but that was physically impossible. They tripped in and out
of my room, demanding that I go and have a drink here or a coffee
there and I became more and more depressed knowing that much
of the reason for their high spirits was my win for our team and yet
here I was, spoiling their evening. Janet tried to tell them I was
tired, but they are irrepressible girls and that did no good at all. In
the end I asked Sheila and Pat Cropper to come in and sit down and
told them, too, what had happened. I begged them to say nothing
to anyone.

They sobered up in the time it takes to flick out a light-switch.
Both of them said, 'Don't go back. Come to live with us in England
until you get yourself sorted out.' I told them I would be returning
to Belfast. They said good night and I never heard another sound
that night. Nor, in the months or years that followed, did those
girls ever reveal a word of what I had told them.

It was about one a.m. when I got into bed. I was absolutely
shattered. I had probably slept a total of about five or six hours over
the three previous nights and a number of unusual things had
happened over that period. I was asleep as my head touched the
pillow and I slept solidly and dreamlessly until ten a.m.

*Mary had been sleeping roughly three of those nine hours when, about
250 yards away at 31 Connollystrasse, in the Olympic Village, an*

Israeli wrestling coach named Moshe Weinberg went to answer a knock at the door of his team's sleeping quarters. Suddenly he shouted, tried to slam the door shut and was shot dead through the woodwork by a Black September gunman. Behind him Joseph Romano, Israel's best-known wrestler, reached for a knife. He was shot dead in the middle of the room. The Olympic siege had begun.

Janet Simpson woke me up and said come over to her room for a cup of coffee. We made it and went out on to the balcony. We looked down on to the most amazing scene I have ever witnessed. The entire Village was ringed by soldiers with automatic guns. It was as though world war three had been declared during the night. We crossed the corridor and went into my room. The first thing we noticed was that all the piped music had been shut off. Then that the streets of the village, normally thronged with people of every shape and colour, were almost deserted. And finally that out there, down the Connollystrasse, there were men crouching on every rooftop. Some had guns and some binoculars or radios. We must have been the last two people in Munich, even in Europe, to learn of the dreadful things that had happened that night. There had been no written warnings for the Israelis.

It was a long, awful day. Most of the British girls were taken out of the Village for a ride around the local sights but I went into town and joined Buster and a couple of other friends at the Diplomat Hotel. Someone bought a transistor radio and through the afternoon we listened to the description of the scene back in the Village where the terrorists were still holding the rest of the Israelis hostage. After dinner I went back to the Village and it was there I heard that the terrorists had been shot out on the airfield at Fürstenfeldbruck but that the Israeli hostages were safe. Like most people I went to bed almost happy.

The next morning I awoke with a nervous rash on my legs. I knew what it was because I had suffered from it before, but I thought I would go across the Village to the team headquarters to check up with the doctor. As I was leaving someone told me that the previous night's news had all been a mistake. The Israeli hostages were all dead. As it happened the memorial service for them was being held in the Olympic Stadium at that very moment. The Village was a ghost town. No one knew whether the Games would continue or not. It was bewildering to athletes who had been preparing so long for events that now may not take place.

For the rest of that day I made plans to leave Munich. It had always been planned that I should return to Belfast before the end of the Games. There was much to be done back in Buster's gym and though, at one time, I would have liked to have stayed for the closing ceremony, there was now nothing to keep me. I knew the *Belfast Telegraph*, who naturally knew nothing of the charming message threatening to make life somewhat difficult for me if I came back, were planning some kind of an official reception. 'Can you come on Friday,' they asked. So I did.

It was an unusually routed journey to Belfast and for the first few hours I could not understand why. First we took one plane across to Frankfurt. Then we were whisked into another plane at the very last minute to London. It seemed rather a roundabout route. In London we came down the steps from the plane to quite a large reception of people I had never seen before and were taken straight from the tarmac to the VIP room where some welcome drinks appeared. We were just having a second drink when a man said to me, 'Were you conscious of what was happening as you got off the plane?' I didn't know what he was talking about. 'Well,' he said, 'I'm pleased about that. But every yard of the way you were surrounded by security men. In fact there was a woman photographer there and at the very best all she could have got was a quick snap of the back of your head.'

It would be stupid to pretend that I had put the message from Belfast completely out of my mind. I hadn't. I didn't like it, but I was going back there anyway because it was my city, my home and the place I loved best. But it was fairly obvious that some people were taking the threat very seriously indeed. Our flight to Belfast was called but nobody moved. Not in our party, anyway. A minute or two before the plane was about to take off we were asked to collect our hand-baggage. Then, in a rush, we were shepherded out to the plane where Buster and I were the last to board. We were taken to seats right at the front and, again, it was not until we landed in Belfast that I learned that the placid looking gentlemen sitting immediately behind us were from the Special Branch.

I understand their concern and I am grateful for it. There would have been a certain amount of criticism, I suppose, had I been shot.

Anyway, they were taking no chances at this stage in the proceedings. It was a curious homecoming. The plane taxied up to the far end of the airport buildings and all the other passengers were asked to leave first from the rear exit. I found myself apologising to everyone for all this inconvenience. All the airport, I discovered later, had been sealed off to the public except those who held special passes. Yet outside I could see that a red carpet had been laid out from the front steps of the aircraft and that a band was waiting. Jay Oliver, from the publicity department of the *Belfast Telegraph*, came aboard, introduced himself and told me what was going to happen next. 'When you go down those steps,' he said, 'someone will be waiting to give you a bouquet. Just say hello, collect the bouquet and keep walking. There's no time to talk to anyone and there's certainly no time for interviews. We've got a gold Rolls Royce waiting to drive you into the city.'

I did exactly as I was told. As I went down the steps the band were playing *Congratulations* and among those waiting at the bottom was Margaret, Buster's wife. We kept walking until we came to the gold Rolls Royce. 'From this point,' said Jay Oliver, 'there has had to be a small change of plans. We've had a man out all night putting posters on practically every lamp-post between here and Belfast saying "Welcome Home Mary." Unfortunately you won't see any of them. For security reasons we're going in by a different route.'

And so we did. We doubled back down country roads which I never knew existed, flying along between hedgerows at a breath-taking rate. When we got to the city the first stop was at Buster's gymnasium. Outside they'd hung up gymnastic rings in the form of the Olympic symbol. Inside the members presented me with a radiogram and the staff gave me a gold bracelet, the first of many lovely gifts I was to receive over the next few days. The ever-thoughtful Jay Oliver whispered a piece of advice. 'Mary, this is the last time you're going to be near a loo for hours. It's going to get pretty hectic from here.' It's one of the things I love about Northern Ireland. Most of the people get their real priorities right.

Jay wasn't exaggerating. The Rolls was still waiting to take us down to the *Telegraph* office where there was lunch, a champagne reception and another presentation, this time in the form of a gold brooch shaped like the switch-back roof of the Munich stadium. Then it was back out into the fresh air for the drive down Royal

Avenue to the City Hall.

Until this moment I had only seen anything remotely resembling a ticker-tape welcome in films about American war-heroes returning to their home towns. Belfast, that afternoon, matched anything I had seen in the cinema. The confetti came down from the office buildings and up from the streets and there were thousands of people who all looked happy, but they were nothing like as happy as I was. We drove slowly along in a lorry with its sides stripped down and I leaned over the edge to let anyone see and touch the medal that Northern Ireland had brought away from the Olympics. It wasn't mine, it was *ours*. From time to time I noticed that the lady constable and several policemen who had been attached to our party weren't exactly looking relaxed about the security aspects of the arrangement. After all the precautions on aircraft, at airports and on the drive in to Belfast it was somewhat contradictory, I suppose, to be driving along on an open vehicle. I've only thought of that since. At the time I simply didn't care.

At the City Hall they had opened the main doors so that we could walk through to another reception. A sentence like that would mean nothing at all in Bradford or Bristol or Baltimore or Brisbane or any other city you can think of beginning with the same letter. In Belfast, where they just didn't open the main doors at all because of the troubles, it was an historic moment. I made a speech there which was quite emotional. It summed up everything I had felt driving along that great street of this great city which, for all its problems, is my eternal home.

So it went on. We went to the Europa Hotel, the tall white building near the station which has become so familiar to practically every newspaperman in western Europe, for a press conference. The chef had baked a cake depicting the five events of the pentathlon. We went to Ulster Television where a studio assistant asked me to remove the bracelet I had just been given because it would flare under the arc lights. I only discovered the real reason half way through our live interview when they suddenly produced yet another bracelet and presented it to me then and there. It seemed that every hour was a Christmas day and it occurred to me that what I had said to Mr Heath was even truer than I'd thought. Belfast *had* been waiting for a happy day. The security people followed us out to Buster's home, where I was staying for the next

To Mary, congratulations from Rowel Friers

She's got the whole world in her hands

Above: This was the moment the long wait ended and I knew that I had won.

Above right: A congratulatory cartoon by Rowel Friers. The caption read: 'She's got the whole world in her hands'.

Right: Heidi Rosendahl came over to congratulate me. In the background you can see the Russian girl whose gamesmanship earned her a sharp dig in the ribs.

Top: On the victory rostrum after the medal ceremony with Heidi Rosendahl and Burglinde Pollak who was quite overcome by the occasion.

Bottom: As it was said when this photograph appeared, I was 'the only person who could outsmile Ted Heath'. You can just see Buster in the background.

Above: The moment of glory on our return to Belfast and the wonderful reception in Royal Avenue. The *Belfast Telegraph* had made these little flags which said 'Welcome Home Mary' on one side and 'Mary Peters' Track Fund' on the other. All the people had ransacked the town for confetti and tickertape and there was no more to be found anywhere. I remember being surprised at the number of people I recognised in the vast crowd.

Left: The back page of the *Belfast Telegraph* the day after I won the gold medal at Munich.

Above: This was the famous moment when Princess Anne gave me the BBC Sports Personality of the Year award which she had won the previous year. I said, 'Hasn't she kept it clean' and it was clean too!

Left: The reception given by the *Daily Express* when I won their Sportswoman of the Year award. With me were all the medal winners from the Munich Olympics.

few days, and then they withdrew. Their job was over. We were on our own. No one had been hurt. I hadn't needed the advice contained in that message to Munich advising me to 'say something about bringing the people together.' Bloody hell, I'd just been running my guts out for everybody, including myself. What more did he want?

That night we went to the Ulster Arts Club and a somewhat spidery entry in my diary records that I went to bed at three a.m.

We took the Europa's lovely cake to the Multiple Sclerosis Society and a lot of the bouquets out to the Glencraig School for Handicapped Children and by the Sunday, with the Olympics still going on in Munich, I was back at work. I really meant to see the closing ceremony on television the following night but someone insisted we all went out for yet another celebration and I missed the whole lot. 'To bed,' says the same diary, 'at four a.m.' It isn't the winning of an Olympic gold that tests the stamina, it's what happens afterwards.

There are some stories that Mary Peters is diffident about telling in case it appears that she sees herself as an amalgam of Joan of Arc, Florence Nightingale and Sister Anna. This is one of them. Five days after her triumphal ride through the streets of Belfast she flew to Liverpool to join her father who was visiting relatives and friends before returning to Australia. Just as she was leaving she received a telephone call from a member of the International Athletes' Club pleading with her to compete in a heavily sponsored meeting at Crystal Palace, London, the following evening. She was now the biggest attraction in British athletics. How she handled the situation, and what transpired, is a small anecdote but a large insight into her character.

I was a bit narked. The meeting had been planned for some months, but I hadn't been invited to take part. Now, all at once, my name was in the headlines. As it happens, I'm a member of the International Athletes' Club, but that didn't commit me to dropping everything and running at their beck and call. I said I was going over to Liverpool to say goodbye to my father and that I couldn't make it. He pleaded with me on the telephone. 'In that case would you just come down to Crystal Palace and make a public appearance? Don't run. Just come and show yourself to the crowd.' I weakened.

I said, 'All right, I'll come if my father agrees to come with me.' I telephoned my father in Liverpool and he said he would join me. It turned out to be one of the more interesting trips of my life. In Liverpool there was a civic reception in the afternoon and a family party in the evening. We were going to look in at the Crystal Palace in between.

We left the reception and caught the 5.15 plane from Liverpool. We sat at the back so that we could slip off first, but somehow the IAC had got a message through that we were being met. We *were* let off first, only through the front door. For the second time in a week I was apologising to fellow passengers for the privileged treatment. As we went forward along the aisle Daddy waved to absolutely everyone. It was like travelling with President Nixon.

A Rover was there to meet us and take us from Heathrow to Crystal Palace. As the crow flies it is only a short sprint on the Home Counties map. As anyone who knows London's South Circular Road in the Friday night rush hour will confirm, it can feel like the proverbial slow-boat ride to the Republic of China. In any case, our timing was right. I had to be at the stadium by 7.25 p.m. And I had to be away again by 7.30 in order to make sure of catching the 8.45 plane back to Liverpool for the party with all those aunts and uncles and cousins. I had asked the airline if they could possibly hold the plane for us in case we were a little late. They said they could hold it for fifteen minutes but not a moment more.

Ray Roseman, who was driving, did a marvellous job, but there was nothing he could do when we hit a solid jam of traffic at a roundabout just short of Crystal Palace. We couldn't move forwards, backwards or down any side road. It was then that I spotted a police car just ahead of us. I told Ray and my father to follow me if they could, jumped out of the Rover and dashed up to the police car in what must have looked like an action-replay of my 200 metres final. It happened to be a little white two-seater sports job with two quite large policemen inside. I tapped on the passenger window. The passenger policeman wound it down and I was still gabbling away about my predicament when a great grin came over his face. 'Ah, Mary,' he said, 'jump in.' MGBs are not large and I'm not built like Margot Fonteyn but I squeezed in somehow and sat there on his lap with my arm round his neck.

We took off. There is no other description for it. Heaven knows how we got in and out of that traffic but suddenly we were at the gates of the stadium. There stood a large police inspector. My new friend wound down the window, cleared his throat and said, 'Actually, sir, Miss Peters here has a bit of a problem, sir. You see . . .' Policemen are wonderful. 'What are you waiting for then?' asked the inspector. Away we went again and they delivered me right at the top of a flight of stairs leading down into the arena where Emlyn Jones, director of Crystal Palace, was waiting. I had two minutes to spare and in that time, to my delight, Ray Roseman and my father caught us up.

My father had my handbag in one hand and my coat in the other and, like that, we went out into the centre of the track to the microphone. I said a few words to the crowd, held up the medal from which I was now becoming inseparable and explained that we had to dash away. We got back into the Rover, headed back through the traffic jam and got to London Airport only five minutes after the scheduled time of our plane's departure. As good as their word they had waited for us. Obviously we had had nothing to eat. In Liverpool we stopped the car on the way from the airport to the party at a fish and chip shop and arrived eating plaice and chips. I worked it out later that the time between my entering the Crystal Palace athletics track and leaving it was something well under four minutes.

12. Life and Death

The four-minute smile at Crystal Palace was only the start of a hectic four months on the celebrity circuit. During this time Mary received more than 7000 letters, commuted to England twice and sometimes three times a week, received award after award, made more television appearances than any British politician, was in constant demand to open things, auction things and say things, was lured by the familiar formula into becoming the subject of This is Your Life *and generally became so instantly recognisable that merely to walk down a street, any street, was to run a gauntlet of autograph hunters, well-wishers and back-slappers.*

There's no doubt that the four months after the Olympics were even more exhausting than the four months before them. Beforehand I was at least getting the nine hours' sleep I had convinced myself I needed, but that was now impossible. I was lucky to get five hours, let alone six. I still had a full-time job to do at the gymnasium and there were all those letters to be answered. A lovely girl called Harriet Duffin rang me up out of the blue one day and said she guessed I would have a lot of correspondence and that she'd be very happy to give me a hand. She typed almost every reply in her own spare time. We became very close friends and I asked her to come over to London with me on one of my many trips. We were walking through Soho one evening when I happened to be wearing my very swish new black cape and hood. A gentleman who appeared to have certain diversions in mind stopped right in front of me, peered under the hood and announced his disappointment at what he saw. 'Now,' he said, turning to his companion, 'there's a real virgin for you.' 'That's no virgin' replied his mate, loftily. 'That's Mary Peters.' Day in, week out we were enjoying giggles like that.

So far as I can remember I only heard one disapproving voice all that time. This was back in Belfast where the Lord Mayor, Sir William Christie, opened up the City Hall again for a civic reception in my honour. People from every section of the community were there and I was invited to take myself along to Lunns, the most expensive jewellers in the place, and choose myself a present from the people of Belfast. I had passed the glittering windows of Lunns every day on my way to domestic science college and it had always seemed as remote as Tiffany's or Tahiti. Now here I was going in without either a purse or a cheque book and choosing the most gorgeous gold necklace.

A television station rang me up half an hour before the City Hall reception began and asked if they could have a copy of the speech I was going to make in advance. I had to tell them that I never wrote out my speeches. I've always thought that is rather an over-cautious way of going about things. It's almost certain that a previous speaker will take the very words you were going to say right out of your mouth or, if not, he will undoubtedly make several points which you will have to reply or refer to. I rather fancied my chances as an ad-libber, anyway, but at this reception I met my match when across the room, accompanied by his wife Eileen, came the Great Preacher himself. Towering of figure, commanding of voice, hair, chin and dog-collar gleaming, the Reverend Ian Paisley generously offered his congratulations. But then came the commercial. In that powerful County Antrim accent which must have made sinners quake out in the street he added, 'Mind you, Miss Peaders, me onlah regrat is that you should have seen fit to have dinnat on the Sabbath Day.'

It was later clearly explained to Mr Paisley, I gather, that Miss Peaders had not been in the position in Munich to rearrange the entire Olympics track and field programme so that the second day of the pentathlon should not fall on a Sunday. But that, I also gather, did not stop Mr Paisley repeating his disapproval of my abuse of the Sabbath when he went to work on his own church congregation the following Sunday. I wasn't actually there to hear it but that's how the story went.

I liked Mrs Paisley. She appeared to be the quieter member of the family and was very sweet and asked me for my autograph for her children. Since it was a weekday I happily obliged.

The Lord Mayor told one story that brought tears to my eyes. Apparently one Belfast person became so excited watching the television transmission from Munich that he rushed out of the house, full of joy and inspiration, and decided to hurdle over his gate. Unfortunately he caught his foot in the top of it and fractured his leg.

In London, of course, the award-of-the-year season was just starting and I must say the critics and the panels and the adjudication committees were very kind to me. I don't regard any of these awards as having any greater value than the other, but the one which certainly has the biggest audience is the BBC Sports Personality of the Year show which goes out live from the BBC Theatre in Shepherds Bush to many millions of viewers. The name is genuinely a complete secret until Frank Bough gives that sunrise of a smile and announces it simultaneously to the winner and the country. Naturally I knew I was on the short list, but so were several others including Richard Meade who had performed so brilliantly in the equestrian events in Munich. In fact the honour came to me and Northern Ireland and I received the trophy from Princess Anne who had won it the previous year for her riding in the Badminton three-day event.

I was a little surprised at how nervous she seemed when she came on to the stage to present it and it was partly because of this that I made the remark which I have been trying to live down ever since: 'Hasn't she kept it clean.' It seemed to lift the tension just a little and as soon as the live show was over we chatted away like old friends. I realised then how entitled she is to feel somewhat apprehensive every time she speaks off the cuff in public. It doesn't matter what I say since I am responsible only to myself. But every word she utters is noted down and analysed for a double meaning.

We were joined on the stage by Henry Cooper, who is the loveliest man you would meet in two careers in sport. 'Good evening, Yer 'Ighness,' said Henry, who by now could afford to set up eight elocution schools, but sees no earthly reason why he should pretend he wasn't brought up in the East End, 'I've just 'ad me car stolen.' Happily Our 'Enry got his gleaming new Mercedes back undamaged, but not before Princess Anne expressed her sympathy and recalled her own bad moment in motoring. Only a little while previously she had been stopped for exceeding the speed limit on a motorway and became the subject for enormous publicity in the press. 'I wouldn't have minded,' she said, 'if there hadn't been an item on the very same page in one of the newspapers about a driving offence which led to a person's death. That was worth only one paragraph, it seems, while I got half a page.' She was angry about that. I agreed with her then and I agree with her now.

Incidentally, a year later when it came my turn to hand the BBC trophy over to Jackie Stewart, the racing driver who had just retired, I said that he, too, shouldn't have much trouble keeping it clean as there were a couple of dusters in the box which had impressive little crests in their corners. It is astonishing how many people really believed that Buckingham Palace dusters bear royal insignia. They don't, of course. I was kidding. The only inscription those dusters bore was a very patriotic 'Made in England.'

Another major award was that given by the *Daily Express*. Gordon Banks, the England goalkeeper who had recently lost an eye in a car accident, was voted their Sportsman of the Year while I won the Sportswoman of the Year title. Unhappily Gordon couldn't be present as he was still recuperating and the *Express*, who were anxious to avoid a presentation lunch without either of the award-winners present, asked me to come over to London the previous night in case we should be grounded by fog in Belfast the following morning. They didn't stint the hospitality. Margaret and I were booked into a suite in the Savoy which could have comfortably housed the entire Household Cavalry, horses included. There were two bedrooms, two bathrooms, a drawing room furnished with the most gorgeous drapes and antiques, a colour television and a telephone in each loo. The windows looked out over the Thames and the moment we arrived a massive floral arrangement was brought in for us to enjoy during our very brief stay.

I was no longer the little girl checking in to the Cobden Hotel in Birmingham in her school uniform, but there were moments when I felt like it. 'Yos, modom?' demanded the lady at reception while she eyed my scruffy overnight Puma bag as though it contained a full set of rusty abortion instruments. 'Peters,' I said. She consulted a list which appeared to meet with her approval. 'Delighted to have you with us, madam,' she said in the sort of voice that she might just as well have used in the first place.

Despite the profusion of telephones in our suite Margaret and I kept dialling things like 0, 9 and 1 in the hope of hearing someone at the other end confess that they were actually room service. This was our own stupid fault because apparently the Savoy is wired up with a series of secret bells which you push to bring liveried servants running at any hour of the day or night. Since our requirements were no more demanding than two cups of coffee we decided to give the staff a night off and go downstairs and get them ourselves. After going down and along for about half a mile we were courteously told that coffee would be served in our suite. By the time we got back they were just wheeling in a table covered by such acres of crisp white linen that if we'd hung it out of the window the entire Savoy would have taken off down the Thames and beaten the *Cutty Sark's* record along the trade winds to India.

There's more to winning a gold medal, you may gather, than meets the eye.

The *Express* lunch was a great success. I sat between Sir Max Aitken and Mr Jocelyn Stevens, proprietor and managing director respectively, with Miss Jean Rook, the famous lady columnist, in close attendance. It was such high-powered company that I didn't like to confess how I'd spent half the morning. I'd been ringing secret bells all over the suite in an attempt to get back the shoes which I'd put out for cleaning the night before. My shoes had genuinely got muddy when I stepped in a puddle at Belfast airport on the way over and my early unbringing insisted that I could not appear anywhere until they were shining again. My father always judged people by the state of their shoes, particularly around the heels.

Going down in the lift I knew the day was going to be a huge success. The lift boy said, 'Ow you doin', Mary?' and suddenly we were in a descending cube of Belfast. He came from the Shankill Road.

The *Express* trophy certainly requires more cleaning than the BBC's. It is as big as a birdbath and massively impressive. When the meal and the speeches were over they wanted pictures of me holding it and it occurred to me that maybe this was what all those years of weight-training had really been for. Their ace photographer sprang on to a window-sill and stood there, legs straddled wide, camera glued to face, in the all-action pose of his honourable pro-fession. It really was jolly unsporting of someone to shout at that moment, 'Hey, *****, did you know your flies were open?' They weren't, of course, and nor did the subsequent pictures suffer from over-exposure.

There was only one disappointment. I have a great affection for Gordon Banks and I wanted to talk to him afterwards on the telephone so I asked the Stoke City manager if he would be kind enough to give me the number. He did so on my solemn promise not to pass it on so that Gordon would not be disturbed by other calls. Unfortunately it was the wrong number anyway.

Life was all so hectic that at one stage in the proceedings I didn't even have the time to go out and buy any new clothes. I would work at the gym while Margaret would go to a store, pick out a selection of dresses and bring them back for me to choose from. I couldn't keep turning up in the same outfits and the invitations were still pouring in. One of the really memorable ones was from 111 Squadron of the RAF, then stationed near Ipswich. They were absolutely whacko-o over the moon about the fact that the number I'd worn back and front in Munich had been the same as their squadron's and they asked Buster and me to fly over to East Anglia for a day as their guests. They wanted to do everything in supersonic style and planned to pick us up in a jet. This was scotched by a Civil Servant. They then asked the Royal Naval fliers near Belfast to fly us over. This, I gather, was scotched by the same Civil Servant. They weren't to be beaten. We eventually went over in a Comanchee and had a glorious day. Out of deference to both the Civil Service and the RAF they would only allow Buster and me to 'fly' in simulators but it was great fun. Dinner in the mess that evening included a sweet named Pentathlon Mousse.

Before the RAF it was the *Bruce Forsyth Show* where my medal caused something of a small sensation when it was discovered that the reverse side bore a kind of relief map of two fairly well-endowed gentlemen standing about without any clothes on. After the RAF it was Eamonn Andrews and his big book in *This is Your Life*. They trapped me going into Bowater House in Knightsbridge where Marea Hartman then had her offices. They give you an hour or so to compose yourself after the initial shock and all that while I was wondering only one thing: had they brought my brother, John, over fom Australia? Lots of friends and relatives appeared, but I really was disappointed when John suddenly came up on film, talking from outside his home in Sydney. Then right at the end of the programme there was a voice that literally made my heart miss two beats. Around the corner of the set came my only brother whom I'd not seen for twelve years. That was the best of very many good days.

A typical period of forty hours around this time was as follows: fly Belfast–London and catch a plane immediately for Newcastle, do a television interview with David Vine and catch the night railway sleeper back to London. Roll off the sleeper, totally dazed, and get out to the airport. Fly London–Belfast and pick up a car at the airport to go out to Carrickfergus, a lovely little seaside place, to present the Town of the Year Award for the best-kept place in Northern Ireland. Join Buster to attend an afternoon meeting of artists, writers and actors and listen to Joseph Tomelty talk like an angel and then return to Belfast for dinner with friends. So, as a somewhat more distinguished diarist once said, to bed. Only with the alarm set for six o'clock the following morning to start the same routine all over again.

Bruce Forsyth had wanted to know if the medal was solid gold? It isn't. It's gilt silver dipped in gold. By the time I had walked out into the stadium in Munich to receive it, it already had my name and my discipline – in common language, my event – engraved round the rim. I can hardly remember anyone wanting to see my Commonwealth Games golds for which I had worked so hard. Everyone wanted to see and touch my Olympic medal. So many that I took to carrying it around with me in my handbag.

One morning, going into the gymnasium, I stopped as usual at the army barrier at the end of Upper Arthur Street. A young soldier with a beret and a flak-jacket and an automatic gun stepped out from his wooden guard post with its sandbags and whorls of barbed wire, and gave me a thorough twice-over with that piece of electronic machinery which is known locally as the geigercounter. Each time, while hovering over my hand-bag, the instrument emitted a high-pitched protest. The soldier gave me a cold, hard, mistrustful look and said, 'There's a large lump of metal in there.' I was mortified. There were a number of people close around me waiting to be electronically frisked. I dreaded being questioned further and then made to open my bag to prove it wasn't a gun. I said, 'It's a medal.'

It rang a bell somewhere in the soldier's mind. He looked at me again and I knew he recognised me. Fatigue and strain were engraved on his face. He didn't enthuse or smile. In a flat, dead voice he said 'Pass on.'

The incident was extremely good for me.

Somewhere, perhaps reading The Times *in a deep leather arm-chair in London's clubland or pouring himself a large scotch in some eminently desirable residence in the stockbroker belt, is a well-spoken gentleman whose urbane composure may be disturbed for one fleeting second if he ever discovers that he appears, albeit briefly, in the autobiography of Miss Mary Peters. He set the seal so completely on that autumn and winter of gold medal celebration that I have gently twisted Mary's arm to relate in public a story which, in private, she adores.*

We had flown over to London for yet another party and yet another presentation, this time as guests of the Sports Writers' Association who had elected me their Sportswoman of the Year. We danced and talked and drank a lot and were in no mood at all to go back to the hotel when the last waltz was over. So we drifted out into the night, myself, Buster and his wife, Margaret, and two friends, Deryck and Malcolm. We strolled around in the hope that there might still be somewhere open where we could get something to eat. It was about two o'clock in the morning and we were getting nowhere fast when we saw advice coming our way in the shape of an elegantly-dressed man. Given three guesses I might have identified him as a surgeon, or a banker or someone rather superior in the Foreign Office. His accent matched his appearance exactly and he was extremely friendly when Buster begged his pardon for stopping him and asked him what London had to offer in the way of food at that time of night.

'Let me see, now,' he said, shouldering his umbrella and concentrating visibly. 'Bit of a problem, actually. There is a little place down there where you might get some greasy bacon and eggs, but I can't say I'd really recommend it.'

He thought again for several seconds and then his face suddenly lit up with inspiration. He looked at Margaret and me in our evening dresses and turned to Deryck who was linking arms with us. 'I've got a very much better idea than that,' he said. 'Why don't you take these girls back to the hotel and **** 'em.'

With a cheery 'Good morning' he was gone as we stood there helpless with laughter. We seemed to laugh our way through all that autumn and winter. We had worked and we had won and every day was Christmas day. It was one of the happiest periods of my life.

In the early hours of the following Easter Tuesday morning Buster McShane had a drink with a friend in the first floor bar of the Arts Club. When he left he climbed into his Jaguar and drove out towards his home. Half way there his car left the road and struck a stone wall. Buster died instantly.

It was about 7.30 on the Easter Tuesday morning when the phone rang. I wasn't even at home. Holiday times had always been rather lonely times for me in Belfast, having no family there, and I had gone to stay with Tom and Flora Craig, two good friends who, like me, originated from Liverpool. Somehow the police had traced me there. I took the call. Would I go immediately and see Margaret, Buster McShane's wife? Yes, of course I would, but why? And then they told me.

It must be difficult for anyone to recall immediate reactions to extreme shock but in my case, amid the confusion of thoughts, was the predominant one that it simply wasn't true. It *couldn't* be true. Buster was a survivor, a winner, a man who dictated his own fate, the epitome of life and living. I knew him to be an impulsive, aggressive driver but for all that he was a very good one with the instant reactions of a very fit man. Anyway, he had promised to telephone me himself that morning to see how my ankle was. We had trained together on the Friday and I had sprained it when I hit the stop-board doing 52 feet, just as I'd bragged to him I would. And what about yesterday, only yesterday? I'd been having a long-lie in at the Craig's when Buster had phoned and got me out of bed to watch a programme on television. It was the prototype of those Superstars sports programmes from Florida where men like Rod Laver and Joe Frazier and Bob Seagren tried their hands at sprinting and swimming and bicycle racing. I had enjoyed it so much that I telephoned Buster back and thanked him for letting me know it was on. 'Okay,' he'd said, 'I'll talk to you tomorrow.'

And now it was tomorrow. And as I stood there, comprehending at last what the police were asking me to do, I knew that this no longer was some nightmare and that Buster was really dead.

Buster's closest friend, Deryck Monteith, came to collect me in his car. On the way out to Margaret's we called at Buster's mother's home. We had to break the news to her because she hadn't heard of his death. Nor, yet, had Buster's children for when we got there they were still asleep. So that terrible day began. There was neither time nor cause for me to think about what it would mean to my athletics career, but when eventually I did it was to cave in beneath our misery and decide there was no point carrying on. Then I asked myself what Buster would have done and two weeks later I competed in a small meeting at Newham. There were hundreds of children there and they all queued up for autographs.

Children mean a great deal to me, particularly the children of Northern Ireland. I had a certain plan in mind that might in some way help them and I knew that Mary Peters, athlete, could achieve it more effectively than Mary Peters, mourner. Buster had wanted me to carry on until the Montreal Olympics in 1976 when he thought I would be at my very peak. I reasoned that I might do quite well in Montreal but that Pollak of East Germany would have been improving all the time and would probably beat me in the pentathlon. But ten months away lay the Commonwealth Games in Christchurch, New Zealand. There I wouldn't be competing for Britain. I would be competing for Northern Ireland. Buster would have wanted that. So I decided to stay in training and go there for one reason only. To win a gold medal that I now wanted very badly indeed. Then I would quit.

A number of slightly varying estimates have been made at the number of Belfast people who stood outside the crematorium hall on the day of Buster McShane's funeral. The lowest, for a city not unacquainted with sudden death, is 10 000. There were certain unusual aspects about the service that took place inside. There were no hymns for the man who painted hymn numbers as a boy. Nor were there prayers. The music heard by the congregation was the Clancy Brothers' rendering of 'I am a Freeborn Man' and a lilting and lyrical song the opening line of which was 'Raindrops are falling on my head.' The first was chosen because the words had had a special meaning for Buster and the second because it was a tune he had liked. Those who would regard this as vulgar are the same people who would have described the playing of

'Onward Christian Soldiers' as hypocritical. The address, a small masterpiece of English and perception, was given by Larry McCoubrey, who had only recently narrated a film about Buster's life for BBC Northern Ireland television and who himself tragically died a year later. The wreath sent by Mary Peters consisted of a precise circle of golden flowers. It bore the inscription 'My medal for you.'

13. Building for the Future

Thirty-two nights before Buster McShane's accident four British soldiers returned with two girls to a ground floor flat in one of the so-called better residential areas of Belfast. The soldiers had met the girls some time previously in the Woodland Hotel in Lisburn. The girls promised them a party and arranged it for the evening of Friday, March 23, 1973. By the time the soldiers turned up their hostesses had already made their preparations. They had provided plenty to eat and plenty to drink. While one served drinks the other said she would slip out and bring back two other girl friends to make up the party. As promised she returned with two newcomers who were unknown to the soldiers. They were men. One carried a Thompson sub-machine gun and the other a pistol. They ordered three of the soldiers, all sergeants, to lie on a bed. The man with the machine gun then murdered all three with bursts of fire through the heads and thorax. Exactly what happened next is difficult for civilian sources to determine. The fourth soldier, severely wounded, managed to crawl to the front door and reach some five yards down the path before collapsing to his right over a neighbouring fence. This meant he was half lying in Mary Peters' property when she drew back the curtains of her living room. Mary had been lying in bed, watching television, in her ground-floor bedroom when the gunman or gunmen fired. Had you been able to pass through one wall to draw a straight line between her bed and the bed on which the sergeants were lying, the distance, give or take an inch, would have worked out at eighteen feet.

It had been a hectic week. I had worked in the gym every day and been out every night and I was very tired. I went home, locked the door and awarded myself the ultimate luxury of doing absolutely nothing at all. My flat is so arranged that by leaving the door open between the living room and the adjoining bedroom, and swinging the television set round, I could lie in bed and watch TV. I have no idea what programme was on that night. All I know is that I was so tired I was dozing, jerking awake, and then dozing again. It must have been around eleven o'clock when I decided I had to make the effort to get out of bed and switch the set off. I did so and then, by some habit which I still have today, I went to the window and drew back the blinds a little to see what kind of night it was outside.

The horror which I saw there was so dreadful that for a few moments I could not take it in. A soldier was lying in the pathway. There were armed troops in my garden and groups of policemen both there and in the garden next door. Immediately outside was an ambulance with its light flashing. And in the dim light behind and around there seemed to be hundreds of watching faces. They weren't moving, just watching. This, at first, was the thing which struck me as being the most horrible of all. But I stayed at the window myself and as I did so three stretchers were brought out and placed in the ambulance.

The crowd hardly diminished. I went back into the bedroom and switched on the radio. Eventually, around midnight, a local news station began putting out a bulletin. They reported a multiple shooting in Cedar Avenue and began to fill in the first details of a crime so bestial that within a matter of hours it was putting Belfast back in the headlines all over the world. Where, in the name of anyone's God, was it all going to end?

I didn't live in the Avenue the bulletin named but it was just round the corner. There could not have been two such incidents as this in a single night. It then struck me that I had heard not a single sound. Had the television been turned up loudly? No it had not. Had I been dozing? Yes, but hardly sleeping soundly. And how much noise did exploding guns make? I didn't know. Yet I had heard nothing at all. Not a sound.

Eventually I went back to bed. I was hardly a novice to the violence of Belfast which I had seen at close and long range before. But I was not unshockable. I slept fitfully between then and dawn and when I woke it was with a feeling of misery and absolute despair. Then a more personal reaction set in. There were still soldiers in front of my house and occasionally they spoke to the early morning passers-by on their way to work. Then I heard one say, 'You know who lives here?' He mentioned my name. From that moment I stayed away from the front window. I dressed quickly but why I don't know. I knew less than the average radio listener in Australia knew now about what had happened in the house next door to where I was now standing, yet I knew I would be pursued. It was one of the lesser rewards for having competed in the Olympic Games. What could I conceivably add to the objective coverage of so terrible a night? Nothing. But I knew that it would be hard to persuade certain branches of the media that that was the case.

I had to go to work. Eventually, around nine-thirty, I left the house, trying to cover my face as I went down the path. I got half way across the road to the bus-stop when I heard someone shout, 'Well, have you got your medal with you *today*?' There was a BBC television crew on the far pavement and within a few seconds of arriving at the bus-stop they were behind me. There was a gentle tap on my shoulder. I knew they had a job to do and I am always sympathetic to any professionals who are answerable to bosses who sit back in the warm comfort of base and make the decisions. But on this occasion I pleaded with them. I suppose they had good reason not to believe me when I said I had seen and heard nothing, but I said, 'Please, please don't implicate me in all this.' Perhaps it is quite possible to be very cool about these things in Surbiton or even Chicago but Belfast in the seventies was a slightly different story.

I do not know whether that BBC crew shot any footage of me or not, but I was terribly upset. I got to the gymnasium, where I was now among people I knew, and I broke down and cried for the first time since I had drawn back the curtains and seen that gruesome scene. I then telephoned the BBC and asked them not to use anything about the fact that I lived next door. It was shortly after this that we all removed the street numbers from our doors or gateposts. Later that day a number of newspapers phoned for interviews. There was nothing I could possibly tell them and I refused to speak to them. Buster spoke to them instead and begged them not to mention that I lived next door. He cancelled an engagement for me that evening, took me home in his car and waited with me until I felt prepared to go inside. It was not that I felt any particular danger. I knew only that I had to get over the ordeal of spending the coming night in that flat alone. I did so, of course, and have lived there ever since. One totally insignificant detail has puzzled me ever since. When that neighbouring room was finally cleared of its horrendous evidence, a single unshaded electric light was left burning from the centre of the ceiling. One year later, to the day, it was still alight. I had no idea that light bulbs could survive so long.

There are many illusions one could give of Belfast violence. Of how on the night of dreadful Bloody Friday I learned a lesson about the stupidity of bravado by leading two waitresses from a restaurant straight into crossfire. Or, on the night of the Abercorn Restaurant bombings, how I phoned Crystal Palace in London to cancel my visit to a weekend get-together of pentathletes. I just didn't want to go. It wasn't that by staying in Belfast I could do anything, but someone, I thought, had to stand fast. Someone had to do something normal in this absurdly abnormal city. It was the weekend after the killings next door that we decided to redouble our efforts to build a new running track for the youth of Belfast.

It is complete distortion to portray the average young Belfast teenager as a street-corner psychotic pelting rocks into over-tolerant ranks of British soldiers. I don't know where the successive television crews round them up from. Maybe its the same ones every time. What, of course, is terrible for every Belfast teenager is that they simply cannot lead a normal life. By simple things I mean going to cinemas, theatres or a football match, taking a girl out or training for sport. If the Munich victory gave me any privilege which I valued above all others it was the opportunity to draw attention to the abysmal standards of athletics training facilities in my home town. In fact 'abysmal' is virtually an exaggeration. There were practically none. If one told an East German or Australian or Canadian athletics official that Belfast did not have a single usable artificial surface running track he would look at you and assume you were suffering from shell-shock. They are damn nearly as common round the world now as tennis courts. But not only didn't we have one in Belfast, we didn't have one in the whole of Ulster and nor was there one anywhere in Southern Ireland either. There *had* been one owned by Queen's University of Belfast, but virtually over one winter it cracked and erupted and soon became dangerous for training and out of the question for competition. The kindly Queen's University had allowed me at least to train there for

Munich and now I had the chance to give something back.

It began with a telephone call to Munich, the day after my win, from Malcolm Brodie, sports editor of the *Belfast Telegraph*. Malcolm has no provincial hang-ups: he's a pale, dynamic character who will pop up in Moscow one day, Paris the next and Rio the following week if there's any big soccer being played there. 'Listen, Mary,' he said. 'We want to set up a fund to commemorate your victory. Don't know where the hell it's all coming from but the first suggestion from the Northern Ireland Women's AAA is that it's a scholarship deal. You know, pick out the most promising youngsters and get them over to England for a few weeks' training and coaching away from all the tensions here.'

Instant answer: 'Good idea, but no.'

Why did we always have to send people to England? Couldn't we do something for ourselves for once? Couldn't we organise some-thing that certainly hundreds, probably thousands, could enjoy each year in our own town? Here was our chance to stand fast, not to run. There was another point. In twenty years in athletics in Northern Ireland I had never known any argument in any dressing-room or committee-room which had been caused by religious or political differences. Why should we be modest about that? Looking round, it seemed a damned good achievement. *That* was what I wanted.

Buster agreed. So did the *Belfast Telegraph*. I am delighted to know that, since then, a scholarship idea is being introduced as well, but from that moment the track almost became an obsession. By the time I got home the newspaper had already printed thousands of flags saying 'Support the Mary Peters Track Fund.'

The site was no problem. The Queen's University track, some three miles out of the city centre, was set among hills and trees and had banking round it to make it a natural amphitheatre. Down below ran the River Lagan. All we had to do was persuade the educational authorities to let us make a start. In fact, they were delighted. They had put aside £15 000 to repair the track surface but that, I knew, would barely look after the back straight. Yes, they would be delighted to add their £15 000 to our fund and agree that in future all sections of the community would have free access to the track.

The first sum we thought we would have to raise was £60 000, but ambition and inflation almost doubled that within a matter of months. We might as well build in as many training facilities as possible while we were about it, and we certainly had to bring it up to the standard where, at last, major track teams would come and visit us from abroad. So the final target became £100 000.

Somewhat cynically I thought of Mr Avery Brundage and his £35 million collection of Chinese jade. Or of the money that went up in smoke every night in Belfast. We could work miracles with only a fraction of that. Even so we had our own excitement as envelopes came in bearing twenty-five pence from an old-age pensioner, ten pence from a school child. That really *was* money. I'd never been involved in fund-raising before and, anyway, I'm completely dumb about cash which comes, I suppose, from never having had enough to get concerned about. It was a long time before I realised that although I was dashing madly about picking up cheques, sometimes five pounds, sometimes twenty-five pounds, from youth clubs and Women's Institutes and Rotary Clubs and schools, it was going to take an awful long time to raise £100 000 that way.

We then had a breakthrough in getting publicity for the track in England. In the space of a week I appeared on a BBC 2 programme, *Voices of Sport*, in which I was able to talk about what we were trying to do, and then we received a sympathetic half page about the project in the *Daily Mail*. The paper was hardly off the presses before I received a call from Geoffrey Wolfe, chairman of Wolf Electric Tools in West London. He said he would like to help. He gave £1000.

That was but one of many, many contributions from *Daily Mail* readers, but it really gave us the encouragement we needed. What I now wanted was the same kind of reaction in Ireland. Already I had been to see Mr William Whitelaw, secretary of state for Northern Ireland, who had not only been one of the first to send me a telegram in Munich but had given a party for me at Stormont Castle on my return. He was a fearfully busy man under enormous pressure, but by enlisting the help of Denis Howell, M.P., then out of office as Minister of Sport but soon to return in the 1974 Election, and also ringing a girl friend of mine, who happened to be Mrs Whitelaw's personal secretary, I got the meeting. Mr Whitelaw is charm itself. He received me in a chintzy, comfortable room in Stormont and had his secretary there taking notes. I had taken along several jagged-edged samples of the broken track we were trying to replace. Almost his first words were, 'Your track cannot be a memorial to Buster McShane.' I thought he must have been misinformed about something. I explained that I just wanted a track – the name of it didn't matter – and that since most governments in most countries would have provided one anyway, and since enormous sums of money were being spent on restoring the destruction in Belfast anyway, it did occur to me that the government had some responsibility. He said he would talk to the appropriate authority, the Ministry of Education. And so he did.

On November 15, 1973, the Northern Ireland Office issued a press release simultaneously in Belfast and London. It began: 'Lord Belstead, Parliamentary Under Secretary of State for Northern Ireland, today announced that the Ministry of Education is to make a major contribution to the Mary Peters Track Fund. Following a meeting with the organisers of the Fund, the Minister said the Government was prepared to contribute £1 for every £1 subscribed by the public. . . . It is expected that this could result in a total Government contribution in the order of £30 000.'

It was a jubilant moment. The idea which had started from a single brief telephone call from a Belfast newspaper to Germany was now underway. We launched a new big appeal in Northern Ireland and by March of the following year a £5000 contribution from John Moores, the boss of Littlewoods Pools, took us to the half-way mark of £50 000. Between my meeting with Mr Whitelaw and then, however, a little matter of the Commonwealth Games in New Zealand had been a distraction.

At a certain point in 1973 I'd just had to put the shutters up against any further public appearances and settle down to the really hard grind of training all over again. All the time I was doing it one point was nagging me. I knew I'd left it too late. You cannot be casual about preparation for the big ones, and without Buster to control my life for me I had this dreadful feeling that now, when I wanted to win so badly, I'd messed it all up.

14. *When the Running had to Stop*

The Tenth Commonwealth Games were staged in Christchurch, New Zealand, a few miles inland from the point where the tall ship Charlotte Jane *had landed the first English settlers 124 years earlier. For Mary, who was now competing in her fifth Commonwealth Games, the distractions and external pressures were unrelenting. Her success in Munich, the death of her coach and her Belfast background, with its overtones of violence, made her an object of curiosity as well as admiration. She could have spent most of her nights, as well as days, giving interviews to newspapers, radio and television reporters. Watching her from close range it was fascinating to observe not only how she kept her composure in the face of these remorseless demands but how she concealed her misgivings about her own lack of preparation for what she had now decided was to be her last appearance in international athletics. The radiantly confident girl who waved and blew kisses to the English-speaking world at the opening ceremony was, in fact, closer to winning an Academy Award for acting than a medal for running, jumping and throwing.*

I had never felt so lonely or unhappy before any big event because every way I turned there were faces or situations which reminded me of Buster and Buster was dead. There were many tears throughout that trip at moments when I found myself alone. There had been no one to drive me through those training schedules and now there was no one to tell me precisely what to do and when. More than that, there was just no Buster, roaring and laughing and slapping people and telling bawdy stories and belting through every day in overdrive. The world was a much emptier place.

It was the time to turn to friends. Deryck Monteith, who had been Buster's closest pal, flew out from Belfast, and Bill Cook arrived from Bermuda. They knew, instinctively, how I was feeling. So did Mary Toomey, in whose shadow I had lived so long as an athlete. She invited me to stay with her in California and train there, far away from the tensions and grey skies of Belfast, for a couple of weeks before going on to New Zealand.

Mary was now on her third surname which is why a few readers may not have recognised her as the Mary Bignal of the late Fifties or the Mary Rand who had taken second place to my fourth in the Tokyo Olympics. It was there, when she was married to Sidney Rand, the rower, that we became very close friends. Her private life is none of my affair but, like many other mutual friends, I was somewhat shocked to pick up a Sunday newspaper one week-end and read that her marriage had broken up. It was only later I was to discover that I had introduced her to her second husband. In 1967 we had both gone to Los Angeles as members of a Commonwealth team to compete against the United States. One night I went to a party given by several American decathletes at a glorious house they had overlooking the beach at Santa Monica. One of them was Bill Toomey who was soon to become the Olympic decathlon champion in Mexico. At a banquet after the match was over Bill sought me out and asked me to bring Mary back to the beach house for another party. I introduced them, we all squeezed into Bill's sports car and for my pains Mary and I finished up having the only almighty row we have ever had.

At some point in the proceedings I can remember driving off to an all-night supermarket with an American 400 metre runner in search of anything that might be cooked up into a combination of dinner and breakfast. We came back loaded with hamburgers and eggs and, unfortunately, a king-size packet of potato crisps. We went into the kitchen where Bill and Mary were deep in conversation. Mary looked up and told me to go and get lost. I was so annoyed that I ripped open the potato crisps and emptied about a dollar's worth over her head. I was then led away to an armchair and ordered to behave myself and go to sleep. At sunrise, with the party still going on, I got up and made breakfast for everyone except Mary. It was the point of no return. She laughed and apologised, I laughed and apologised and we agreed that our mutually appalling behaviour the previous evening may have been the result of what *Private Eye* magazine delicately refers to as 'overtiredness.' We'd certainly had a few drinks. Of such collisions are lasting friendships made apparently. Mary married Bill Toomey after the Mexico Olympics and on her way to California was photographed by the world's press at Amsterdam airport wearing, by way of disguise, the kind of wig you associated with Louis XIV rather than one of the most beautiful girls ever to appear on an athletics track. She was never one to do anything by halves.

Now, in mid-December 1973, the Toomeys opened their home to me in America. Bill, in charge of physical education at the University of Irvine, was in training to take part in the latest American TV Superstars production. He was also coming to New Zealand as a representative of Chevron, the firm which had built the new running track in Christchurch, and bringing Mary with him. For me it was a wonderful stroke of luck. I had been trying to keep to the training schedules which Buster had set me for the Olympics, but I needed personal contact, too, and Mary was an inspiration. In California she came out and tried to beat me at everything in our first training session and was scarcely able to walk the next day. She also coached me in the long jump with such effect that I came very close to the 20 ft mark which I'd never yet achieved.

Immediately after Christmas Mike Bull, the Northern Ireland pole-vaulter who had also been trained by Buster, arrived and we stayed with John Forde. But then the weather turned bad. After three days of stair-rod rain we sloshed our way to a travel agent, changed all our schedules and caught the night plane to New Zealand. We were the first athletes to arrive in the Commonwealth Games Village and were greeted by the kind of meals the Dorchester would be proud to serve.

I had never been to New Zealand before and found Christchurch full of surprises. It had streets as wide as New York, but was still virtually a country town populated by friendly, worthy, sensitive people used to living life at a leisurely pace. It was rather like going into one of those late Edwardian homes where the discipline was never questioned and no one ever seemed to do anything just for the hell of it. I was astonished, for example, to find a town packed with overseas visitors still shutting all its bars at ten o'clock in the

Left: On my return from Munich Harriet Duffin helped me reply to over 7000 letters and is accompanying me here at one of the many receptions we attended.

Below left: This was the day I received my MBE from the Queen at Buckingham Palace in 1973. We had quite a chat and I asked about Princess Anne who had been injured and she told me that she was in training again.

Below right: Back in training again. I have used up to 245 lbs for this exercise. Mike Bull and I helped each other quite a lot in our training and here you can see our shared concentration.

Above: Marea Hartman and myself outside the Town Hall in Christchurch with the beautiful fountains in the background.

Above right: The hurdles in the 1974 Commonwealth Games. I won my heat and was amazed to learn Modupe Oshikoya had won in a faster time.

Right: On the rostrum with Modupe Oshikoya who won the silver medal and Ann Wilson who won the bronze.

Above: After the medal ceremony I met a little girl called Nicola with Derek Murray, the assistant team manager and Dick McColgan (on my left) the team manager. Derek showed her my medal, but Nicola was not at all impressed and said, 'Oh, I have got 45 of these at home'.

Below: This is a photograph taken at the Queen's University track for which the Mary Peters' Track Fund was set up. As you can see the surface is dangerously breaking up.

Top: Following my retirement I have been making a number of
charity appearances. This was a visit to Southport in 1973 with
John Moores of Littlewoods Pools. We took the crippled children
of Liverpool on an outing and had a great day out.

Bottom: At Springhill Primary School in Belfast where they have
560 pupils. Between them they raised £560 for the Track Fund.

evening. I was even more astonished to go into what appeared to be a very smart restaurant with some friends and find the head waiter asking us to pay for our meal before we'd eaten it. No one seemed to eat in restaurants in the evenings and maybe that kind of treatment was the reason. But there were plenty of plusses too. Hundreds of local residents gave up their holidays to drive athletes and officials around, the food in the Village was so good that some competitors actually complained about being offered steak for breakfast as well as lunch and dinner and the security was so tight that for the first time in my memory you could walk around in the Village without being thronged by hangers-on and autograph-hunters. One newspaper report claimed that this was because of the presence of the Northern Ireland team, but I regarded that as nonsense. Tragically, since Munich, all major sports events of this kind have to be protected against all forms of lunatic attack or demonstration and Christchurch did an incomparable job.

For all the milling thousands of people, and the few close friends I had there, these, for me, were still the lonely Games. Curious though it may sound I found it hard, as a member of the Northern Ireland team, to be on chatty terms to members of the English and Scottish teams, even although we had been close colleagues in combined British sides. We were now rivals and I found it as difficult to say 'hello' to them as they did to me. Perhaps Buster's philosophy was getting through at last. You had to be hard.

I was competing in four events, the hurdles, the high jump, the shot and the pentathlon, but in three of them I was doing little more than putting in an appearance. To diversify was to ask for trouble and all my thought and ambition was concentrated on the pentathlon. That was the one I wanted to win and I wanted the gold, if anything, more desperately than I had wanted the gold in Munich. It was scheduled for the first Friday of the Games, the day immediately after the opening ceremony.

Any thoughts that the waiting days and hours might drag were dispelled by the arrival of Deryck Monteith from Belfast. He breezed in full of gossip and good cheer the previous Saturday and the following day came out to watch us compete in a pre-Games meeting. He stood there all day in the blazing sun and it didn't surprise me, therefore, when he complained of feeling unwell in the evening. The next morning when he said he felt worse it became a little perturbing. Ex-Ireland rugger captains don't exactly cave in under the kind of ailments that a couple of aspirins and a large scotch will cure. He went back to his motel to rest, but when I phoned him later to see how he was it was to be greeted with the news that he was seriously ill and that a doctor had been sent for. By the time I arrived at his motel the doctor had been and gone, diagnosing gastro-enteritis. After watching Deryck stare speechlessly at the ceiling for four hours I sent for the doctor again. This time he diagnosed constipation. Early the following morning Deryck was on an operating table in hospital and undergoing surgery for a burst appendix.

It was typical of Deryck that he had no intention whatsoever of missing my last pentathlon, now only three days away. It was also typical of the tough attitudes of New Zealanders that they promised him he would be there provided he could prove to them that he could stand on his feet. I pleaded with the nurses not to let him do anything stupid, but they said keeping him in hospital would probably do him more harm than letting him out for the day. Anyway, the doctors were having bets among themselves about whether the mad Irish dentist could make it. With only twenty-four hours to go I wouldn't have risked twenty pence on Deryck's chances, but next morning he was out of bed at seven o'clock and walking up and down a corridor. The doctors were convinced and gave him parole. Happily Deryck's wife had two friends, Ross and Dorothy Lascelles, living in Christchurch. They borrowed a wheelchair and with the aid of that and a couple of sticks Deryck got himself down to the Queen Elizabeth II Stadium. When I came out through the tunnel on to the track there were Deryck, Bill Cook, Mary Toomey and my father all waving encouragement. My spirits rose considerably.

It would be wrong to pretend that I was at the same pitch of physical fitness that I had been at the start of the Munich Olympic pentathlon. For all that I felt well and in an aggressive mood and was suffering no ill-effects from the previous day when a cold south wind straight up from Antarctica had cut through the stadium throughout the whole of the long opening ceremony. To avoid hanging about in the wind before the ceremony began we'd come to a quiet arrangement with the stadium foreman that I could go and sit in his hut until the march-past began. This plan came unstuck when we got there to find it occupied by a large Alsatian suffering from what I can only describe as canine schizophrenia. We shut the door on him and fled. Luckily, with a couple of Isle of Man athletes, I found refuge in the large tent where the Maori dancers were changing and we sat there on a rug until the ceremony began. It was viciously cold outside and we were only wearing flimsy dresses, but we smiled and waved our way round that track as though it were the most glorious mid-summer's day. It was essential, after all the grim publicity Northern Ireland had had throughout the world, that we showed ourselves to be a happy and united team.

Next morning the wind had gone and it seemed like a perfect English June morning as we drove the six miles across town to the stadium which was set in such rural surroundings that a herd of Friesian cows were munching away in a field only 300 yards from the shot-put circle. But this was hardly the time to ruminate on the glories of nature. One hell of a day lay ahead because for the first time in a major international event the pentathlon was going to be decided in one day instead of two. There had been considerable wranglings about this decision. More than a year earlier I had written complaining about it, but had never received a reply. Taking this silence to mean 'no' I prepared myself mentally for a one-day competition and came to the conclusion that this would probably suit me better anyway. I was big and strong enough to reel the events off in quick succession and I wouldn't have to go through that dreadful torture of a sleepless night in between. Some two months before the Games I was then surprised to receive a letter from John Le Masurier, the English coach, asking me to support a petition to have it changed to two days. This didn't suit my book at all so I replied that I wouldn't. Even so, when I arrived in Christchurch there were still moves afoot to press for the change. I must confess to getting somewhat bloody-minded about it. I was now reasonably experienced in the behind the scenes machinations of athletics. Our Irish team manager went to plead my case at a specially-convened meeting and emerged with a smile which told me immediately that we had won the day. We were now committed to a programme which read: 10 a.m. hurdles, 11 a.m. shot, 1.30 p.m. high jump, 4 p.m. long jump, 5.30 p.m. 200 metres.

As the reigning Olympic champion I was entitled to feel confident, but at the same time I was a little apprehensive, knowing that I had not prepared as thoroughly as these big occasions demand. I knew that the Canadian, Diane Jones, was a very big threat. At Munich Diane had hit a hurdle in the opening event and had been taken to hospital to have several stiches put in the wound. That would have been curtains for some competitors, but she'd returned and put up such a courageous show in the four remaining events that she had still finished tenth overall. I met Diane soon after she'd arrived in Christchurch and, at the risk of sounding feline, was somewhat relieved to hear that until quite recently she'd been suffering from an ankle injury. I knew that Ann Wilson, at her best, could be a real danger, and there was also Barbara Poulsen, the New Zealander. I had an uneasy feeling that a patriotic home crowd could do a great deal to lift her performance. One name that gave me not a moment's concern was Modupe Oshikoya, who was a charming little girl from Nigeria with a warm smile and her hair tied up in spiky plaits. I can't imagine why I should have had such a blind spot about her since she had not only competed at Munich but finished a very creditable fourteenth. Yet I couldn't remember even seeing her there and nor had I read about any of her performances in the athletics magazines. Had the pentathlon come later in the Games I would probably have been more concerned, since it was at Christchurch that so many African athletes emerged in the very front rank of world-class performers. Perhaps my ignorance was just as well because had I known of her capabilities she would have given me a sleepless night. She was certainly about to give me a rather hard day.

I was fairly pleased with my time for the hurdles. It really is vital to get a good start and I was first away in my heat, led all the way and won it in 13·94 seconds. This was the same time as Ann Wilson achieved in her heat and far better than Diane Jones's 14·8 which lumbered her with a big points deficit right from the start. All was well with the world until I looked at the scoreboard again and saw that the unknown Miss Oshikoya had just clocked a very disturbing 13·72 secs. It still left me second overall after the hurdles but it was distinctly bad news. I looked around to pick her out and there she was, very calm and very self-possessed as though she'd been doing this kind of thing since David Livingstone had been down her way. She wasn't big but she was beautifully built and as she warmed up again she ran as effortlessly as a gazelle.

I felt instinctively that by late in the afternoon this girl could be giving me a great deal of trouble in the 200 metres so it was more important than ever that I made it really tough for her now in the shot. This was where I had to build up my points lead. Charlie Stewart, who was there reporting for the *Belfast Telegraph*, told his readers that I was looking very tense and nervous at the start of the shot and he was probably right. But the tension didn't appear to do anything but good. I improved with each of my three throws, building up from 44 ft 4 in to 49 ft 2½ in and then, finally 49 ft 4½ in. For the moment it pushed Oshikoya out of the picture, put Diane Jones right out of the reckoning and left me just ahead of Barbara Poulsen whose best throw was 48 ft 7½ in. We went away for the lunchtime rest with me leading the competition by seventy points from Poulsen.

The first afternoon event, the high jump, did little to change the position except to see Ann Wilson take over from Barbara Poulsen as a big rival. We started jumping at 5 ft 1 in and Oshikoya, Wilson and I all kept going clear up to 5 ft 8½ in. Then, at 5 ft 9¾ in we all failed. Each of us, therefore, added 974 points to our score with the long jump and 200 metres still to come.

Mercifully my first long jump was a respectable one of 19 ft 0¾ in because a long, disturbing wait while the victory ceremony for the 10 000 metres run took place did nothing at all for my concentration. My rhythm was completely gone when I tried to improve on it. In my second attempt I slapped a foot right over the board for a no-jump and my third effort was simply pathetic. My little Nigerian friend had pulled out a beauty and was still looking as cool as if she were just going off to a village dance. There was no Buster to turn to. Mary Toomey had been giving me the thumbs up and Deryck and Bill Cook and Charlie Stewart, the voice of Belfast, had all been giving me signals from the stand, but they will all know what I mean when I say it wasn't the same.

The points now flashing up on the board only confused me. I was still leading on points, but what did it mean in terms of yards and seconds in the final event? I went over to where all the Northern Ireland officials were scribbling away on scraps of paper. I knew by now that I wasn't going to be at Oshikoya's shoulder at the end of the 200 metres, but how much could I afford to be behind her?

The consensus was that if I could hold her to an advantage of between seven and eight yards I would take the gold. I had a lead of 109 points overall and I was so heartened by the news that I can remember saying, 'I'll have to break a leg to lose.'

Well, I didn't break a leg but I nearly burst my lungs. It was a murderously hard run, much harder than in Munich coming as it did at the end of a single exhausting day's competition. I was away well but so was Oshikoya, and all I saw of her after the bend was her back which I dare not let pull too far away. It was a tremendous battle, but as we went over the line I reckoned I was between six and seven yards behind. The electrical devices confirmed it. Oshikoya's time was 24·15 seconds, mine 25 seconds dead. To beat me overall Oshikoya had to win by 1·2 of a second. I had done what I came for and the gold medal was mine.

I was being realistic, not defeatist, when I knew that that was the last prize I would ever win as an athlete. All my mental preparation had been concentrated on the pentathlon and I knew that it was beyond me to key myself up again sufficiently to win any of the other events for which I had entered. Anyway I had subconsciously allowed myself the luxury of thinking that if I justified the long journey with the gold on the opening day then I could ease off and just enjoy the rest of the Games. It is not the way to win. My chances in the shot flickered briefly when I got in the best put in the qualifying rounds, but the old hunger had gone.

My emotions had always been so close to the surface that I was surprised how calm I felt as I walked out across the track to receive my medal from Sir Alexander Ross. Perhaps it was because something had just happened to make me realise how self-indulgent any tears of mine would be.

Immediately after the end of the pentathlon I had heard my name being called by a group of people and went across to the fence to discover who they were. They were partially paralysed and all in wheelchairs. They were members of the Irish paraplegic team who had been competing in their own games in Dunedin only a few days before. They were on the first short leg of the exhaustingly long haul back from New Zealand to Belfast, an excruciating journey for a fully-fit person let alone anyone who was physically handicapped. Yet they had insisted in getting off their plane at Christchurch and being brought out to the stadium so that they could see me competing for the last time. They were bubbling with fun and so happy for me that I almost had to force myself to realise that every one of these people had been stricken with a deep personal tragedy. I wondered how I, who had often regarded a pulled muscle as the end of the world, would have faced up to such a challenge. These were the gold medal winners of an altogether bigger game.

Athletics, all forms of highly-competitive sport, can become small, insular worlds at times. It is good to be brought back to reality. It happened to me again only a few hours later. After all the interviews and the champagne I went back to the Village and as I was coming out of the dining-room I met a little girl wearing Scottish national dress. Derek Murray, our assistant manager, lifted her up, discovered her name was Nicola and then said: 'This is Mary Peters and that's the gold medal she's just won.'

Nicola looked at the medal and then at me. 'Well,' she said, 'I've got forty-five of those at home.'

Two days before the Games ended there was another shock, this time with no humour about it at all. I was taking some friends out to lunch when Maeve Kyle stopped me and asked if I knew which flight Mary Toomey had left on that morning to return to America. I wasn't sure and asked why she wanted to know. 'There's been a plane crash,' said Maeve, 'but at the moment we don't know anything more than that.' Two flights had taken off from New Zealand for America that day and one of them, the Pan American, had crashed at Pago Pago with what was reported to be a heavy loss of life. Several London newspapers had open lines to their reporters in Christchurch and the reporters were frantically trying to get the two respective passenger lists. For two hours I was quite speechless. Before leaving America for New Zealand I had heard Mary's, daughter, Samantha, continually saying, 'You *will* be safe, Mummy, won't you?' and Mary laughing and reassuring her in that carefree way she had about everything. After two hours the news came through. Mrs Toomey had left from Auckland that morning by Air New Zealand. I just don't know what I should have done had the answer been otherwise.

The Games closed on a Saturday before almost the whole British Royal Family and 34 000 other people. Justifiably the whole stadium had erupted when Filbert Bayi, from Tanzania, broke the world 1500 metres record, but for me the main recollection of that final afternoon in athletics was of the totally unfair conditions under which the women high-jumpers had to compete. I was one of them, but on this occasion I was not concerned for myself because I knew I wasn't going to win it. Curiously, perhaps, I had struck up a great friendship with the very youngest competitor, the Australian Debbie McCawley, and she was only one of those consistently being hampered by other athletes who were either running on the track or waiting around to do so. I thought I had seen nearly everything there was to see during a long career in sport, but the lack of consideration shown that afternoon by some athletes to others simply amazed me. Again and again the high-jumpers were having to break off because of people standing in their line of approach or actual track events passing in front of them or metallic announcements coming over the loudspeakers just as they were running in with total concentration. It was hopeless. I protested very strongly about it and I hope it was the last time we shall ever see organisers try to combine an important field event with track events on a final day. There were many excellent aspects of the Games organisation in Christchurch but this certainly wasn't one of them.

My annoyance may well have been a blessing in disguise. It certainly prevented me from becoming over-nostalgic, maudlin even, about the fact that this was the last time I would walk out into an athletics arena with that familiar half nervous, half elated feeling which you never lose before big competition. Down all the years I had nearly always had that optimistic feeling that this was going to be the day when it all came right, but now there was some inner conviction that another medal was beyond me. I was really only competing because I knew that Buster would have wanted me to. I spent most of the competition chatting to Debbie McCawley. At 5 ft 8 in, well below what I had achieved in Munich only fifteen months earlier, I knocked the bar off. I knocked it off a second time. When I knocked it off the third time the announcer solemnly announced that my career was over.

Few athletes in modern times have established a greater rapport with crowds than Mary Peters. She always made them feel like one of the family. She was demonstrative, extrovert, warm, emotional. Her last exit was totally out of character. She gathered up her clothes, hurried across to the steps that went underground to the locker-rooms, looked

briefly up into the panorama of faces in the great cantilever stand,
waved once and was gone. Just like that.

I could hardly wait to get away and nor was there to be any coming
back. Had Buster lived I would probably have continued for
another three years until the 1976 Olympic Games in Canada, but
I knew that without him there was little chance to do so with success.
It had to be a clean break.

There was one final honour to come in that arena. Mike Bull had
carried the Northern Ireland flag at the opening ceremony. I was
to carry it at a closing ceremony which was to prove less informal
than sheerly chaotic. Only the previous evening one of our Ulster
boxers, the flyweight Davie Larmour, had won a gold medal. When
the guard of honour came to haul the Ulster flag up to the masthead
the rope had jammed and it refused to budge. I was determined to
make up for that by seeing that our flag was now the highest in the
closing parade. I went and found the biggest man at the Games, the
twenty stone Canadian shot-putter, Bruce Pirnie. I climbed on to
his shoulders and he carried me right round the track with the flag
held high above my head.

Larceny isn't normally my game but I badly wanted that flag as
a final souvenir. Towards the end of our circuit I pulled it down
and gave it to one of our badminton players, Dorothy Cunningham.
I asked her to try and sneak it back to the Village for me as I would
clearly be a prime suspect once the officials had discovered it was
missing. Dorothy kindly agreed to try and I forgot all about it until
I returned to the Village where the all-night farewell celebrations were just beginning. Marea Hartman invited us over to the
English women's quarters for champagne and as I was leaving their
block I suddenly caught sight of Dorothy, still clutching that flag.
She had a policeman at one shoulder and a policewoman at the
other. I dashed across to start the explanations when the policeman
beat me to it by saying, somewhat gravely, 'I wonder if you would
ask all the Northern Ireland ladies to gather in one room, please.'

I had an awful feeling that on my very last day I had caused real
trouble for all the team. When we were gathered together the
policeman said: 'I am sorry to have to say this, girls, but would you
be kind enough to go and search all your luggage. You see, there's
been a bomb scare.'

The man must have thought I was mad for I suddenly heard myself saying loudly, 'Thank Christ for that.'

It was a hoax. There were no bombs at my last of the Friendly Games. We sang and danced and drank and laughed the night away and when the sun came up I was Mary Peters, the former athlete. I still have the flag at my home in Belfast. It's folded away in a drawer until I can think of the right place to hang it.

15. Home is Belfast

In the eight months between writing the first word and the last chapter of this book Mary Peters and I were both fortunate enough to travel round the world – separately, though meeting occasionally – doing pleasant things like dining alongside one of the world's most beautiful fountains in Christchurch, New Zealand, drinking rum punches in Trinidad and dry martinis in Sydney, gambling gently in Macau's casino and, in my case, looking at the girls' legs in Tahiti. The point of mentioning such an idyllic existence is that there is no reason why Mary should not continue to do this, or something like it, for the rest of her days. She would have to work her passage, since she is not wealthy, but her talents and friendships are such that she need never again set her feet in the city of Belfast which, during these eight months, went from bad to the brink of civil war. She would be lionised in her native Liverpool, fêted in London and welcomed back, as a member of any profession, in any city in which she has ever appeared as an athlete. Many people have tried to persuade her to do precisely this, but without a hope of success. They are met with the usual smile and the words 'No, I'm going home, thank you.' Home is not only the house next door to the flat in which three men were assassinated. It is also in that part of Belfast which, according to plans captured in May 1974, was directly in the path of a proposed scheme to burn down houses of innocent, apolitical and unbigoted people around their ears. Mary Peters will not be moved.

There is a world of difference between dejection and despair. I am frequently dejected to the point of tears at what has happened to Belfast. I have never despaired and never shall. It is quite true that the situation has deteriorated considerably during the period in which we prepared this book but to despair, to give up fighting for a solution or the restoration of sanity, is to give up hope and that is the creed of nihilism. I *know* there is goodness in the hearts of the people of Northern Ireland because I can walk through the streets of the Falls and the Shankill and see it every day. Since my retirement from athletics I have been approached to go into politics, both by members of the Conservative and the Alliance parties. But politics, professional party politics, is not my way. I am not a political animal. My philosophy is simply that life is very precious and that every hour of every day must be lived positively. This is the outlook we have lost in Belfast: the feeling that there is little point setting oneself a target to achieve because we do not know what disaster tomorrow is going to bring. It is this attitude I want to work and fight against. It may sound pompous for me to say that this was the example I tried to set on the running track but it is true. Deliberately, everywhere, I ran in the name of Belfast and Northern Ireland to attempt to show the world that our spirit was not dead. I know that my efforts were not wasted on the ordinary people at home. I have received a number of titles in the past two years. I have been made a Member of the Order of the British Empire and I have had conferred upon me the title of honorary Doctor of Science by the New University of Ulster for what they saw as my work for 'community relations.' I am greatly honoured by both, but the title I really prize is that of 'Our Mary' which is how I am often greeted by people of all section of the community. A few days before writing these final words we stood in the recently-bombed Royal Avenue of Belfast selling flags to raise more money towards the running track which I so anxiously want to see built. We collected £400 in small sums in a very short period. People of all faiths and outlooks literally queued to give money. They believed in the project and it is days like that which give me hope and encouragement.

My life, in the few brief months since leaving athletics, has changed beyond recognition. For the first time in more than twenty years I have time. I have time to clear the three foot high weeds out of my garden. I have time to make cushion covers. I have time to cook a proper meal instead of opening tins. I have time to invite people in to have dinner with me and time to go and visit friends I have neglected for years. Until now time was something that only other people had. My own life was an unending rush from work to

track to training to meeting with just a few minutes in between to
snatch a meal or a shower. There was certainly never time for a
holiday because holidays were something you saved up to go away
to the Commonwealth or the European or the Olympic Games.
Time is the most luxurious commodity there is and I am luxuriating
in it, not by wasting it but in using it in different ways.

After New Zealand there were so many things I wanted to do with
my new freedom from training and athletics that, reluctantly, I
decided to give up working at the McShane Health Club. I had
enjoyed many happy years there, but suddenly a new world was
opening. I came back from those final Commonwealth Games to a
mountain of invitations and I wanted, selfishly perhaps, to be free
to accept them. There was an invitation to go to Canada to appear
in two television programmes. There were invitations to make a
public appearance here, to open something there, to advertise this,
endorse that, try my hand as a comments 'expert' with the BBC and
London Weekend athletic reporting teams on television. I didn't
exactly see myself as the distaff David Coleman or the package-deal
'personality' for hire, but some of these offers promised me the freedom which I wanted to enjoy. Anyway, I thought I had earned some
of them. Almost every year I had travelled further than any other
British athlete. I had competed in more pentathlons than any other
woman athlete in the world. So I threw in my job and trusted to luck.
I wanted to earn just enough money to keep my head above water
and leave myself time to continue my activities in Belfast. Apart
from raising the final money for the new track I have quite a few
other commitments, like being a member of the Sports Council and
the Northern Ireland BBC Advisory Council. I value these positions
greatly as being platforms for expressing the views of my generation.

Money for personal possessions or luxuries doesn't worry me
greatly. It rarely does to people who have never had any. Inevitably
I gave away all rights to pensions and superannuation when I quit
teaching, so Buster and I jointly bought a large house in Belfast
which was designed to give me some kind of assured income if I
were ever to reach old age. Obviously nothing is assured in Belfast
any longer. Although I have lived, and continue to live, in the house
myself the other three flats it contains have remained empty for a
long while. You can never be quite sure these days who your
tenants are likely to be. Nor has the value of property exactly

increased in our street. There are few prospective buyers for a house next door to where one of the most terrible crimes of the Troubles took place. In fact, I find myself living in a house of no value at all. This is a roundabout way, I suppose, of saying that if you see me doing things like advertising certain products on television I shall be earning my keep, not just 'cashing in' as so many sportsmen and sportswomen are accused of doing.

The solution, as I'm sure you will have decided for me already, is to go and get married. I am continually being asked why I am not. The question was put to me once right out of the blue on a television interview and a friend of mine was so outraged by what he regarded as the impertinence of it that he had to be restrained from challenging the interviewer to a duel to the death. I didn't find the question either impertinent or embarrassing. I am not married for the age-old reason that I have reached the age of thirty-five without the right man coming along. Of course I am sorry about it because I would dearly love to have a good home with a husband with whom I could share everything and lots of children all over the place. But the essential factor of that lovely existence has to be the right man and until such time as he comes riding over the horizon on his horse and takes my breath away I shall remain single. I don't at all rule out that it can happen, but I am certainly not getting married for the sake of security. I have seen too many marriages collapse under the strain of the constant travel that sport demands to be blasé about such an institution. I shall never become one of those housewives without many outside interests, but I do know that I am now at the stage where I would happily surrender part of the self-sufficient life I have led for years.

It is inconceivable that I should end this book on such a serious note. I would prefer to remember, as one does as the evening draws on in a bar, just a few of the crazy and embarrassing stories that one confides to close friends after one drink too many.

Like the warm glow it always gives you when you are recognised in public, as when the lady leaned out of a taxi in London and called, 'Well done, Mary Rand.' I didn't mind at all. I minded even less when she stopped the taxi round the corner and came running back to apologise. 'Do forgive me,' she said, 'of course you're not Mary Rand. You're Sylvia Peters.'

Like the night I appeared on the Russell Harty Show with Omar

Sharif and Diana Dors. When my turn came some voice off-stage began intoning the words 'Twenty years ago this little girl from Ballymena won a sack-race . . .' I'd had a couple so I pulled my long gown up over my knees and hopped across the set to my chair alongside the famous interrogator. It was pretty evident that Russell had been concentrating so hard on his questions that he never heard that introductory line. He looked at me as though I had either taken complete leave of my senses or else had become stricken by some awful affliction which his researchers had forgotten to tell him about. I shall never forget the horror on his face or my own cringing embarrassment.

Like the occasion when the organisers of a filthy-rich social affair in London said, 'Of course we can't pay you a fee for coming over from Belfast, since you're an amateur, but we'd be happy to fix you up with a little Yves St Laurent number if you'd come and draw the prizes.' As the filthy-rich so often do they forgot all about the little number until I reminded them. This provoked nervous coughs and a grudging invitation to go and choose some small memento from the great House of St Laurent. I selected a £20 royal blue silk blouse and a £60 taffeta green skirt and wore both that evening to the great occasion. 'Did you get something?' asked the organiser. 'Yes,' I said, 'I'm wearing it.' '*All* of it?' he cried. 'Yes,' I replied. 'Isn't it beautiful?' and I gave him one of those smiles with which one confidence trickster instantly recognises another.

Like the time I asked for a cab to pick me up at the BBC Television Theatre in London, went down the stairs and had to wait for ages while the taxi-driver simply stared at me without opening the door. Finally it dawned on him. 'Cor, it's Mary Peters. The message I got was to pick up a pair of heaters.' Or the East End kid who was so anxious to get an autograph that he nearly crushed my toes. I found myself shouting 'Get off my foot.' 'What 'ave yer got,' he replied, 'afflete's foot?'

Along the way, through failure and success, great happiness and deep sadness, I have received many thousands of letters. One of them, delivered to the Commonwealth Games Village in New Zealand, was from Mr A. E. Sanders, of 37 Oxford Street, Lyttelton, New Zealand. He enclosed, as a gift to me, a tattered piece of cardboard. 'I have held this,' he wrote, 'for the past fifty-six years and I think it is probably the only one left in existence. It is grubby but that is just some of the mud of Flanders fields.' It was the official Christmas card of the Ulster Divisions serving in France in 1916.

'I am Irish,' Mr Sanders wrote, 'and I am so proud of it that I wouldn't be dead for £1000 a week. We live peacefully here. Ecumenicalism is spreading. We have Roman Catholic bishops preaching in Anglican cathedrals and vice versa. When Catholics have a night out, Anglicans do the baby-sitting. When Anglicans go out, Catholics look after their homes. May God bring such a peaceful conclusion to the place where you live.'

Those with a God to pray to may wish to read those words again.

Career Highlights

Represented Northern Ireland at every Commonwealth Games
since 1958.

British international since 1961.

1964 Tokyo Olympic Games: Pentathlon 4th
1966 Jamaica Commonwealth Games: Shot 2nd
1970 Edinburgh Commonwealth Games: Shot 1st.
1970 Edinburgh Commonwealth Games: Pentathlon 1st
(Commonwealth record)
1972 Munich Olympic Games: Pentathlon 1st (World record)
1974 Christchurch Commonwealth Games: Pentathlon 1st

Index

Compiled by Hazel Bell

facilities, 8; *1958* Games, 22;
training programme, 60–1;
style 69, 85; Munich Olympics,
80–3; New Zealand, 137, 140
Hopkins, Thelma, 11, 12, 19, 20,
22, 43; mother of, 20
Howell, Denis, 128
hurdles, 12, 61, 68, 69; early
equipment, 8–9; at Munich,
75–7; New Zealand, 136
Hurlingham, shot put at, 40

Ibbotson, Derek, 68, 100
Independent Television News, 97
International Athletes' Club,
109, 110
International Olympic Committee,
20, 33
Ipswich, RAF squadron at, 117
Irish Paraplegic team, 138–9
Irish Republican Army, 103
Isle of Man, 4

Jamaica Commonwealth Games,
49, 51, 53, 58–9
Johnston, Dr Wilson, 54
Jones, Diane, 136, 137
Jones, Emlyn, 111
Jugoslavia, 67; Belgrade, 65

Kemp, Peter, 79
Knowles, Linda, 65–6
Knowles, Teddy, 66
Kyle, Maeve, 12, 20, 22–3, 139

Lancashire, 39; *see also* Liverpool
Larmour, Davie, 141
Lascelles, Dorothy and Ross, 134
Le Masurier, John, 78, 89, 135
Lisburn, N. Ireland, 10
Liverpool, 1–5, 13, 14, 17, 41, 42,
109–10, 111, 143; Victoria

Friendly Society, 2; University
track, 42
London, 110–11, 112, 114–17,
117–18, 119–20, 143, 146, 147;
first visit to, 18–19; Crystal
Palace, 62, 74, 109–11, 126;
Savoy Hotel, 115–16; Soho,
112; West Middlesex Hospital,
54; White City Stadium, 18–19,
39–40
London Airport, 40, 66, 106, 110,
111
Londonderry, N. Ireland, 10
long jump, 12, 61, 132; early training facilities, 8; at Munich Olympics, 86–9; New Zealand, 137
Los Angeles, 37, 131–2; UCLA
track, 72

McBride, Don, 16
McCawley, Debbie, 140
McClelland, Kenny, 6, 7–8, 9,
10, 11, 91
McCoubrey, Larry, 122
Mack, Karen, 78, 92
McShane, 'Buster' (Robert
Terence), xii, 26–38, 39; gymnasium of, 27, 32, 33–5, 37,
106, 107, 112; MP's coach,
32–3, 37–8, 42, 48, 49, 50–1, 53,
58–9, 60–1, 69, 70–3, 76, 78,
81–2, 84–93, 94, 96, 98, 100,
101–2, 103, 105–7, 108, 119–20,
125, 127, 129, 130, 132, 140, 141,
145; death, 120–1; funeral, 121–2
McShane Health Club, 37, 106,
107, 112, 145
McShane, Margaret, 51, 107,
115–16, 117, 119, 120
Mary Peters' Track Fund, 127–9,
144
Meade, Richard, 114